The Oxford First Companion to

The Oxford First Companion to
MUSIC

Kenneth and Valerie McLeish

London
Oxford University Press
New York   Melbourne
1982

How to use this book

All through this book strips labelled *More about* will tell you where to
find out more information about things on a page. Each section of the
book has a letter:

A   Listening to Music
B   Music round the World
C   Instruments and Orchestras
D   Singing and Dancing
E   The Story of Music
F   Composers and their Music
G   Writing Music

The number after the letter is the page number, so D10 means page 10 in
Singing and Dancing, E17 page 17 in *The Story of Music*, and so on.

Where you see this sign you will find suggestions for music to
listen to

Oxford University Press, Walton Street, Oxford OX2 6DP

Oxford   London   Glasgow   New York   Toronto   Melbourne
Auckland   Cape Town   Nairobi   Dar es Salaam   Tokyo
Kuala Lumpur   Singapore   Hong Kong   Delhi
Bombay   Calcutta   Madras   Karachi

© Kenneth and Valerie McLeish (text) 1982
© Oxford University Press (other material) 1982

First published 1982
Second impression 1982
ISBN 0 19 314303 8

Designed by Ann Samuel
Illustrated by Carl Melegari, David Eaton, John Dugan, David Mostyn
Gary Rees, Tony Morris, John Woodcock
Picture research by Peta Hambling, Elisabeth Agate and Carol Cleal

McLeish, Kenneth
    A first companion to music
    1. Music—Juvenile literature
    1. Title II. McLeish, Valerie
    780   ML3930.A2

ISBN 0-19-314303-8

Printed in Hong Kong

Contents

A Listening to Music

Some important words   12

B Music round the World

Music is everywhere   2
Music, magic and religion   2
Music and the seasons   4
Background music   5
Folk music   6
Britain and America   6
Folk music in the 20th century   7
Folk music of the world   8-9
African music   10
West Indian music   12
Steel bands   13
Indian music   14
Music of the Far East   15
Entertainers past and present   17
Music in the theatre   18
Musical shows   18
Popular singers   20
Hits of the past   20
Silent films and 'talkies'   21
Crooners   21
Jazz   22
The instruments of jazz   22
Swing bands   23
Pop   24
Rock 'n' roll   24
Rhythm and blues   25
The Beatles   25
Pop music now   26
Pop films   27
Records and recording   28
Bands   30
Military bands   30
Pipe bands   30
Brass bands   32

C Instruments and Orchestras

How instruments work   2
What is sound?   2
Kinds of instruments   3
Woodwind instruments   4
Flute   5

Oboe   5
Clarinet   6
Bassoon   6
Brass instruments   7
Trumpet   8
Horn   8
Trombone and tuba   9
Other brass instruments   10
String instruments   11
Bowed instruments   12
Plucked instruments   13
Percussion instruments   14
Drums   15
The players   16
Harp   17
Keyboard instruments   18
Keys   18
Plucked strings   18
Clavichord and piano   19
Pipe organ   20
Unusual sounds   21
Electronic instruments   22
Synthesizer   22
Unusual instruments   23
The orchestra   24
The orchestra at work   26
Concerts   26
The theatre   26
Films, television, and radio   27
The recording studio   27
Leader and conductor   28
How a conductor beats time   29
Behind the scenes   30
Soloists   31
Chamber music   32
Kinds of chamber music   32

D Singing and Dancing

Our voices and how we use them   2
What is your voice made of?   2
Vocal cords   2
Throat, mouth, teeth, and tongue   3
All kinds of singers   4
Singing with other people   5
Church music and church choirs   6
Opera   8

What is an opera? 8
400 years of opera 10
Some operas and their music 11
How an opera is made 13
Operetta 16
Some famous operettas 16
Dancing 18
Some dance fashions 18
Hand in hand or cheek to cheek? 19
Some favourite dances of the past 20
Formation dancing 21
Stage and television 22
Dance films 23
Some famous film musicals 24
Ballet 26
The stories of ballet 27
Three ballets 28
How a ballet is made 30
Writing a ballet down 32

E The Story of Music

Music through the Ages 2-3
Ancient music 4
The sounds of ancient music 5
Some instruments from ancient times 5
Musicians at home and abroad 6
The music of ancient Rome 6
The Greek legend of Orpheus 7
The Middle Ages in Europe 8
Christian Church music 8
Music for entertainment 10
The music of the Middle Ages 11
The Renaissance 12
Church music 12
Some Renaissance inventions and discoveries 13
Ladies and gentlemen 14
Madrigals 15
Renaissance music 15
Baroque music 16
Harpsichord and violin 16
Music for the stage 17
Luther and chorales 17
The 18th century 18
Fashions in music 18
Musicians and their employers 19
Freelance musicians 20

Musicians on tour 20
Orchestras and symphonies 20
18th-century music 21
Some inventions and discoveries of
    the 17th and 18th centuries 21
The 19th century 22
Music in the home 22
Romantic music 24
Two popular stories
    (*Faust* and *Romeo and Juliet*) 24-25
Some 19th-century inventions and discoveries 25
Concerts 26
19th-century music 27
The 20th century 28
Music in and out of school 28
New sounds 30
A masterpiece and a riot
    (Stravinsky's *Rite of Spring*) 30
Some 20th-century inventions and discoveries 32
20th-century music 32

F Composers and their Music

Bach 2
Bartók 4
Beethoven 5
Berlioz 6
Brahms 7
Chopin 8
Debussy 9
Handel 10
Haydn 11
Liszt 12
Lully 12
Mendelssohn 13
Monteverdi 13
Mozart 14
Prokofiev 15
Purcell 15
Schubert 16
Schumann 17
Stravinsky 18
Tchaikovsky 19
Verdi 20
Vivaldi 21
Wagner 22
Walton 23

Composers and their countries   24
Dvořák   25
Grieg   25
Wizards of the orchestra
   (Mahler, Ravel, Respighi, Strauss)   26
Gallery of 20th-century composers
   (Britten, Copland, Elgar, Gershwin, Ives,
   Messiaen, Rakhmaninov, Schoenberg,
   Shostakovich, Webern)   28-31
Three avant-garde composers
   (Bedford, Cage, Ligeti)   32

G   Writing Music

The composer   2
How does music get on paper?   3
Writing music down   4
How long or short?   4
Speed   4
Metronomes   5
How high or low?   5
What instrument?   6
How loud or soft?   6
The performer   7
Some words for loud and soft   7
Some words for fast and slow   7
Mood words   7
An orchestral score   8
Unusual kinds of score   10
What kind of piece?   11
Music for orchestra   12
Music for voices   13
Music for soloists   14
Index   15

Acknowledgements

We are grateful to the following for permission to reproduce copyright material:

Music extracts

Boosey & Hawkes Music Publishers Ltd. (*Concerto for Orchestra* and *Sonata for Two Pianos and Percussion* by Béla Bartók, *Pictures at an Exhibition* by Mussorgsky/Ravel, and *The Rite of Spring* by Igor Stravinsky); Durand S.A. Editions Musicales, Paris/United Music Publishers Ltd., London (*Réveil des Oiseaux* by Olivier Messiaen); Henmar Press Inc., New York/Peters Edition Ltd., London (*Concert for Piano and Orchestra* by John Cage); Edward Kassner Music Co. Limited (*Rock around the Clock*); Oxford University Press (*Viola Concerto* by William Walton, and 'Hill an' Gully' and 'Wata come a me y'eye', both from *Folk Songs of Jamaica* edited and arranged by Tom Murray); Joaquin Rodrigo (*Concierto de Aranjuez* for guitar and orchestra); Schott & Co. Ltd (*Artikulation* by György Ligeti); Stainer & Bell Ltd. (*Hymn of Jesus* by Gustav Holst. American rights: Galaxy Music Corporation); Universal Edition (London) Ltd. (*Nr.3 Elektronische Studien, Studie II* by Karlheinz Stockhausen).

Illustrations

Music round the World

Page B1 John Walmsley; B2 (top) Barnaby's Picture Library, (middle) Marian Morrison, (bottom) Douglas Dickins; B3 (top left) Douglas Dickins, (top right) Tony Morrison, (centre left) Will Green, (centre right) Firo Foto, (bottom) Tony Morrison; B4 (top) Barnaby's Picture Library, (centre left) Hulton Picture Library, (centre right) Mansell Collection, (bottom) Camera Press; B5 (top) British Library, (centre) Musée de l'homme; B6 (top) Mary Evans, (bottom) Mansell Collection; B7 (top and centre) Peter Newark's Western Americana (3), (bottom left) Camera Press, (bottom right) Bettmann Archive; B10 (top) Agence Hoa Qui, (centre) Bernard Gérard, (bottom) Alan Hutchinson (2); B11 Agence Hoa Qui (4), (bottom) Barnaby's Picture Library; B12 (top) Ann Bolt, (bottom) Barnaby's Picture Library; B13 (top left) Barnaby's Picture Library, (top right) London Features; B14 (centre) Douglas Dickins, (bottom) Michael Holford/British Library; B15 (centre) Alan Hutchinson, (bottom) British Library, (right) Douglas Dickins (3); B16 Hamlyn Group (2); B17 (left) British Library, (right) British Museum, (bottom) Barnaby's Picture Library; B18 (centre) Mary Evans, (bottom left) Mander and Mitchenson Theatre Collection, (bottom right) Peter Newark's Western Americana; B19 (left) Barnaby's Picture Library, (right) Mary Evans, (centre) Zoë Dominic; B20 (left) Mansell Collection, (right) C. D. Paramor, Suffolk (2); B21 Kobal Collection; B22 (top) London Features, (bottom) Richard Bird; B23 William Ransom Hogan Jazz Archive; B24 London Features; B25 London Features; B26 Rex Features (3), (bottom right) London Features; B27 Kobal Collection; B28 Bettmann Archive (2), (bottom left) Decca Record Company Ltd.; B29 Bettmann Archive; B30 Topkapi Sarayi Müzcsi Müdürlügü, Istanbul, (bottom) Peter Newark's Western Americana, (centre) Ronald Sheridan; B31 (left) British Library, (right) Douglas Dickins; B32 Peter Newark's Western Americana (2), (bottom) Bettmann Archive.

Instruments and Orchestras

Page C1 London Musical Museum; C2 Heather Angel (2); C4 (top) Michael Holford/British Library, (centre) Victoria and Albert Museum, (right) H.M.S.O.; C7 (top) H.M.S.O., (centre left) Mansell Collection, (right) Richard Bird; C11 Michael Holford/British Museum; C13 Richard Bird; C14 Michael Holford; C15 Barnaby's Picture Library; C16 Barnaby's Picture Library; C17 (top) Michael Holford, (bottom) Musée de Versailles/Giraudon; C18 Victoria and Albert Museum (2), (top) Illustrated London News; C19 Victoria and Albert Museum; C20 Barnaby's Picture Library; C22 Chrysalis Limited; C25 Reg Wilson; C26 (top) Boosey and Hawkes/John Foraste, (bottom) Barnaby's Picture Library; C27 Richard Bird; C28-32 Suzie Maeder (12).

Singing and Dancing

Page D1 Firo Foto; D4 (top) Reg Wilson, (centre) Mick Rock, (bottom) Landesbibliothek, Switzerland; D5 (top) E. P. Dutton & Co., Inc., (centre) Clive Barda, (bottom left) Musée des Beaux Arts, Brussels, (bottom right) Mansell Collection; D6 (top) Hulton Picture Library, (bottom) Victoria and Albert Museum; D7 Barnaby's Picture Library; D8 (top) Vision International, (bottom) Reg Wilson; D9 (top) Ove Arup & Partners, (centre) Reg Wilson, (bottom) Giraudon; D10 (top and bottom) Mansell Collection (2), (centre) Hulton Picture Library; D11 (left) English National Opera, (right) Hulton Picture Library; D12 (left) Mansell Collection (2), (left) Reg Wilson (2); D13 (top) Mander and Mitchenson Theatre Collection, (centre) Bettmann Archive, (bottom) Clive Barda (2); D14 (top left) Reg Wilson, (top right) English National Opera, (bottom) Reg Wilson (2); D15 (top) Reg Wilson (2), Richard Wagner Gedenkstätte, Bayreuth; D16 (left) Zoë Dominic, (right) Reg Wilson; D17 (left) Reg Wilson, (right) Hulton Picture Library, (centre) English National Opera; D18 (top) British Library, (centre) Hulton Picture Library, (bottom) Bildarchiv National Bibliothek, Vienna; D19 (left) Mansell Collection, (right) Hulton Picture Library, (centre and bottom) Mary Evans (2); D20 (top) Bibliothèque Nationale, Paris, (bottom) Hulton Picture Library; D21 (top) Hulton Picture Library (2), (bottom left) BBC, (bottom right) Mary Evans; D22 ATV Network Ltd.; D23 National Film Archive; D24 (left) Kobal Collection, (centre and bottom) National Film Archive; D25 (top) Barnaby's Picture Library, (bottom) National Film Archive, (right) Rex Features; D26 (top) British Library, (top right) Royal Ballet/Crickmay, (bottom) Royal Ballet/Zoë Dominic; D27 (top left) Hulton Picture Library, (top right) Bibliothèque de l'Institut de France, Paris, (bottom) Houston Rogers, (centre) Zoë Dominic; D28 (left) Royal Ballet/Crickmay, (bottom) Sadler's Wells/Royal Ballet; D29 (top) Royal Ballet/Crickmay, (centre and left) London Festival Ballet; D30 (top and centre) Royal Ballet/Southern, (left) Royal Ballet/Crickmay; D31 (top) Royal Opera House/Southern, (bottom) Royal Opera House/Williams, (right) Ballet Rambert (2); D32 Royal Opera House/Crickmay; Institute of Choreology, London (dance notation).

The Story of Music

Page E1 Mansell Collection; E4 (top) British Library (centre) Mansell Collection, (right) Michael Holford; E5 Michael Holford; E6 (top) Z.E.F.A., (centre) Michael Holford; E7 Michael Holford; E8 (top) R. Hoppin, (centre) Michael Holford, (bottom) British Library; E9 (left) Museo Nazionale, Naples, (right) Bibliothèque Nationale, Paris; E10 (top) Bibliothèque de L'Arsénal, Paris, (left) Peter Newark's Western Americana, (right) British Library; E11 (top) Bibliotheca Riccardiana, Florence, (bottom) Detroit Institute of Arts, (right) Michael Holford; E12 (top) Hulton Picture Library, (centre) Michael Holford; E13 Giraudon; E14 (top) H.M.S.O. (centre) Cooper-Bridgeman Library; E15 (top) Giraudon, (bottom) Musée des Beaux Arts, Nantes/H.M.S.O.; E16 (top and centre) Mansell Collection, (left) Victoria and Albert Museum; E17 (top) Devonshire Collection, Chatsworth. Reproduced by permission of the Chatsworth Settlement Trustees, (bottom) Mansell Collection; E18 Museum für Kunst und Gewerbe, Hamburg; E19 Archiv für Kunst und Geschichte, Berlin (3); E20 (top) Mansell Collection, (centre) Hulton Picture Library; E21 Mansell Collection; E22 Richard Bird (2), (bottom) Hulton Picture Library; E23 (left) Kunst Museum, Basel, (right) Illustrated London News (2); E24 Mansell Collection; E26 (top and bottom) Hulton Picture Library, (centre right) Cooper-Bridgeman Library; E27 (top) Michael Holford/Museum of London, (bottom left) Richard Bird, (centre) Mansell Collection; E28 (top) John Walmsley, (bottom) Mansell Collection; E29 (top) John Walmsley, (bottom) Barnaby's Picture Library; E30 (top) Ralph Fassey, (bottom) Paul Moon; E31 (top right) BBC (bottom) EMI Ltd.

Composers and their Music

Page F3 (top left) Archiv für Kunst und Geschichte, Berlin, (centre) British Museum; F4 (centre left) Interfoto, Budapest, (centre right) G. D. Hackett, (bottom) Hungarian Embassy, London; F5 Beethoven House, Bonn; F6 (left) Archiv für Kunst und Geschichte, Berlin, (right) Bibliothèque Nationale, Paris; F7 (top) Archiv für Kunst und Geschichte, Berlin, (centre) Snark International; F8 Archiv für Kunst und Geschichte, Berlin; F9 (centre) Arts Council, Great Britain, (right) Snark International, F10 (left) Warburg Institute, University of London, (right) Hulton Picture Library; F11 (right) Mansell Collection (2), (bottom) Hulton Picture Library; F12 Archiv für Kunst und Geschichte, Berlin; F13 (top right) Bodleian Library, (centre right) Tiroler Landesmuseum, Innsbruck, (bottom) Scala International, Florence; F14 Mansell Collection; F15 Mansell Collection; F16 Archiv für Kunst und Geschichte, Berlin; F17 (top left) Archiv für Kunst und Geschichte, Berlin; F18 (top) Mansell Collection, (centre) Hulton Picture Library, (bottom) Glyndebourne Festival Opera/Guy Garrett; F19 (centre) Royal Ballet/Leslie E. Spatt, (right) Novosti; F20 Mander and Mitchenson Theatre Collection; F21 (top) Archivio Storico Ricordi, (bottom) The Royal Collection, London; F22 (top) Crown Copyright, (bottom left) Mansell Collection, (bottom right) Archiv für Kunst und Geschichte, Berlin; F23 (right) Christina Burton, (bottom) Hulton Picture Library; F25 (top) Interfoto Budapest, (bottom) National Museum, Stockholm, (right) Will Green; F26 Archiv für Kunst und Geschichte, Berlin (2); F27 Archiv für Kunst und Geschichte, Berlin; F28 Decca Record Company Ltd.; F29 Mander and Mitchenson Theatre Collection; F30 United Music Publishers; F31 (top) Universal Edition (London) Ltd., (centre) Camera Press, (right) Eric Auerbach; F32 Performing Arts Services, New York.

Writing Music

Page G1 International Freelance Library (Bente Fasmer); G2 (top) Universal Edition (London), (bottom) Boosey & Hawkes Music Publishers Ltd.; G3 British Library; G5 Richard Bird (2); G11 Oxford University Press/Sanford H. Roth.

Listening to music

All through this book, we have given suggestions for listening. Not everyone has the same tastes in music, or likes the same kind of sounds, but we think that the pieces we recommend give a good 'flavour' of a composer, or of a particular kind of music. More important than that, they are enjoyable for themselves. If you are coming to classical music for the first time, try the works on these pages first. Then move on to pieces in the rest of the book that sound interesting, and move on from there.

Usually, if you like one piece by a particular composer, it's a good idea to try some of his other music too. Record companies sometimes issue 'samplers' or 'highlights' records, to give a taste of several different pieces. Try these, and follow up complete performances of the works whose sound you like. If you *don't* like a piece – and some works are harder to listen to than others – leave it for a few months, and then try again. If you can *play* or *sing* with other people, you're luckiest of all. But music is *listening* too – and these pages are a kind of map to show you where to start.

Music to listen to

Peter and the Wolf by Prokofiev
This is the story of a brave boy and a ferocious wolf. Its words are spoken with musical accompaniment. There is a twittering bird (played by a flute), a slinky cat (clarinet), a mournful duck (oboe), and a grumbling grandfather (bassoon). The music is tuneful and easy to follow, and gets particularly lively when the wolf and the huntsmen come along. After this work, try another piece by Prokofiev, the March from his suite *Love of Three Oranges*.

Variations and fugue on a theme by Purcell by Benjamin Britten
This piece is made up of short sections, each one highlighting one of the instruments of the orchestra. You will often hear it called *A Young Person's Guide to the Orchestra*. Sometimes it is recorded with a speaker, telling you which instrument is to play next. The music comes to a particularly clever, exciting finish, where the music from the beginning is fitted over the different music of the end. After you've heard it, try another Britten piece, *Simple Symphony* for strings.

Overture, The Marriage of Figaro by Mozart

This scurrying, four-minute piece sets the scene for a bubbling comedy. The strings have most of the bustle, and the wind and brass instruments play bright fanfares, and the main tunes of the overture. But oboes and bassoons also have a tiny moment of bustle, all their own. If you like the work, try Mozart's overtures to *The Seraglio* and *Così fan Tutte.*

The Sorcerer's Apprentice by Dukas

This orchestral piece tells, in music, the story of a sorcerer's apprentice who tries his master's spells, with disastrous results. The music keeps coming back to two ideas: high, sliding, 'magic' chords on the violins, and a low, bumping tune for the bassoons (taking the part of brooms sent to fetch water). If you like this work, try another piece of 'story' music, Malcolm Arnold's Overture *Tam O'Shanter.*

The Erlking by Schubert

This is a song, for solo voice and piano. (Try, if you can, to hear it first sung in English, or to read an English translation of the words before you hear the record.) The song tells of a desperate father galloping through a stormy night to carry his sick child to a doctor. The child keeps hearing the voice of the Erlking, whispering to him to come and live in his fairy kingdom; the father says it is just the howling and whispering of the wind. In the piano part, you can hear the clattering horse's hooves, and the roar and surge of the storm. If you enjoy this song, try others by Schubert: the bubbling serenade *Hark, hark, the lark,* and the beautiful slow melody *To Music.*

Suite: Scaramouche by Milhaud

This suite for two pianos has three short movements. First comes a rollicking gallop, like a musical picture of roller-skaters, gliding, tumbling, falling round the rink. The second movement is like a gentle conversation, with the two pianos sharing and echoing the same tender tune. The third movement, called *Brasiliera*, is a bouncy South American dance. If you enjoy this suite, try another light-hearted work by Milhaud, the jazzy *Le Boeuf sur le Toit* ('The Ox on the Roof'), a musical impression of a 1920s Paris night-club with that unusual name.

1812 Overture by Tchaikovsky

This music paints an orchestral picture of a huge battle, complete with gunfire and even cannon. Listen for the French national anthem (the Marseillaise), and for the solemn hymn-tune 'Russia' – and also for the rushing strings near the end, when the soldiers make their final attack. If you like this overture, try next the first movement march from Tchaikovsky's *Symphony No 5*.

Water Music suites by Handel

These groups of short pieces were written for royal 'water-parties', travelling down the River Thames. The king (George I of England) went ahead in the royal barge, and the musicians followed after him in another boat. The music works well on dry land, too: minuets, horn-pipes, airs, and gavottes in a cheerful, light-hearted style. If you enjoy it, try another Handel work, *Organ Concerto No 1 in F*.

Some important words

accompaniment   Sometimes you sing or play an instrument entirely on your own (see **solo**). If you perform with other people, and yours is the most important part, the music the others play is called the *accompaniment* (in classical music) or the *backing* (in pop). The person who plays the accompaniment is called the *accompanist*. (See page D4.)

acoustics   The science of sound. If you study acoustics, you are studying how sounds are made, and how we hear them. (See pages C2, C3, D2, D3.)

aria   A song, usually in an opera. The word *aria* is Italian for 'air', and sometimes in older English *air* or *ayre* was used for 'song' as well.

backing   see **accompaniment**

ballade   A piece of music in a particularly fiery, poetic style. Many composers, including Chopin, Schumann and Brahms, wrote ballades for piano.

canon   In a canon, one voice begins the tune, and another voice comes in a little later, singing the same tune. Each part of the tune fits with the other parts. In a **round** (like 'London's Burning' or 'Three Blind Mice') the voices finish the canon, and then begin again, singing the same music round and round as often as they choose.

chord   A group of notes played together.

divertimento   A light-hearted piece with several movements, intended (as the name tells) to divert or entertain. Composers of Mozart's time often wrote divertimentos for playing at parties or while their employers ate. (See page E19.)

étude   see **study**

fanfare   A short tune, usually for brass instruments, meant to catch people's attention. When presidents, kings and queens appear in public, trumpeters often announce them with a fanfare. Modern fanfares (sometimes only two or three notes) are used in airports, or at International Games meetings, to show that an announcement is about to be made.

fantasia   A piece where the music follows no strict rules, but is shaped by 'fancy'. In the time of Elizabeth I, many composers wrote fantasias (often called 'fancies') for virginals, based on popular tunes. 19th-century piano performers played fantasias at their concerts, based on tunes from popular operas. (Nowadays we use 'medley' in much the same way.)

fiddle   A violin used in folk music. Many classical violinists call their violins 'fiddles' as a kind of slang.

finale   The final movement of a piece in several movements.

fugue

A piece based on a short tune or theme, which appears constantly (like a coloured thread running through a piece of knitting). It is often used upside-down as well as right way up, slowed down, speeded up, even played backwards – and the rest of the music is devised to fit. Many of Bach's finest works use fugues, for example *48 Preludes and Fugues* for keyboard. (See page F3.)

lyric

The words of a song, especially in pop.

manual

An organ keyboard played with the hands. (The foot-keyboard is called the **pedals**.) (See page C20.)

melody

Another name for 'tune', in pop and classical music.

movement

When several pieces are grouped together to make a single work (as in symphonies, suites or concertos), they are called *movements*. The movements of a classical work are usually played in the same order every time.

nocturne

French for 'night-piece'. A quiet, dreamy kind of piece. Chopin's nocturnes for piano are some of the best known.

opus

Latin for 'work'. Many composers give each piece an 'opus number': *Sonata Op 13*, for example, means 'My thirteenth published work, a Sonata'. Sometimes several works are grouped together in one opus number: you might see, for example, *Quartet Op 18 No 6*. 'Op posth' (short for 'opus posthumous') means a work published after the composer's death.

ostinato   A beat or tune which keeps on being repeated, whatever else is happening in the music. *Ostinato* is Italian for 'obstinate'. In Ravel's *Boléro* the side-drum plays the same *ostinato* rhythm for 16 minutes (the entire length of the piece). In the Beatles' 'All you need is Love', the same *ostinato* tune (the title) is heard over 100 times in the second half.

prodigy   Someone who shows great talent, usually very young. Mozart, for example, was a 'child prodigy', playing the harpsichord in public at six, and composing from the age of four. (See page F14.)

rondo   A piece in several sections, where the first section keeps coming round again. Many classical sonatas and symphonies have last movements in rondo form.

round   see **canon**

scherzo   *Scherzo* is really Italian for 'joke'. In music, it means a fast, bustling piece in three-time. Many classical symphonies and sonatas have a scherzo as one of their movements.

serenade   Once a serenade was a piece for performing out of doors (often a love song to be sung under a lady's window). In Mozart's time it came to mean much the same as *divertimento*: a collection of light-hearted movements meant for entertainment at parties and picnics.

shanty   A song used by sailors on old-fashioned ships, to help them keep a rhythm as they worked. Many shanties (for example 'What shall we do with a Drunken Sailor?') are still sung in schools and by folk groups.

solo   Italian for 'alone'. When you play on your own, or when your part is highlighted from all the others, you are a soloist, and you are playing a solo. (See page C31.)

study   A piece concentrating on one particular difficulty in playing. By learning it, you train your fingers or voice to cope with that difficulty. Many studies are no more than exercises. But some (for example those of Chopin and Debussy) are good listening music too. Often studies are called by their French name, **études.**

unison   'Together'. In a unison piece everyone plays or sings the same notes.

variations   To play variations, you start with a tune, then make a series of changes to it: decorations, and alterations of every kind. In each variation, the basic shape of the tune can still be heard: it is like basic dough, whatever kinds of fancy loaves or rolls you make from it. For many composers (Mozart, Beethoven, Schumann, Brahms), variations were a favourite kind of piece to write.

vespers   The evening service in Anglican or Catholic churches. Many composers have provided music for parts of the service (especially the Magnificat, 'My soul doth magnify the Lord', and the Nunc Dimittis, 'Lord, now lettest thou thy servant depart in peace'). One of the grandest of all musical Vespers is Monteverdi's *Vespers of 1610*, a two-hour work for soloists, choir and orchestra. (See page F13.)

voluntary   A short organ piece played at the beginning or end of a church service.

Music round the World

Young people entertaining the public in a town shopping centre

▲ Football fans: chanting, shouting, clapping, whirling a rattle

Music is everywhere

Can you sing, or whistle? Do you ever hum, or clap, or dance? Do you watch television, listen to records, go to films, circus, or theatre shows? Can you play an instrument?

When you do any of these things, you are making or listening to **music**. It can be simple (like a football chant, or a playground skipping game), or complicated (like a symphony, or a pop concert by a famous group). It can be serious (like hymns in church and school), or just for fun (like dance music). But whatever its style, and however we use it, music plays a part in all our lives.

If we could listen to planet Earth from outer space, our ears would be filled with piping, whistling, and a pounding, rhythmic beat: thousands and thousands of people, making music of every kind.

Music, magic and religion

The first music in the world was probably connected with magic and religion. It was a way of catching the attention of the gods. Men thought that the world was full of demons and spirits. Some were friendly, and brought good luck. Others were unfriendly, and sent disease or death. It was important to please the spirits and keep them happy – and music and dancing were a way of doing this.

In some parts of the world (for example Papua New Guinea, among remote African tribes, and in the Amazonian rain forest), this kind of music still exists. These people take devil-dances and demon-music seriously, as part of their religion.

Other religions use music too, from chanting in Buddhist temples to hymns in the Christian church. This is not a magic language or a means of avoiding disaster. It makes the worship of God something special, richer than the ordinary words of everyday life. It also helps worshippers to join in the service, and share in the ceremonies the priests perform.

▲ Carnival devil-dance from Bolivia, South America

▶ Demon, witch and dancer from the island of Bali

▲ Tibetan Buddhist monk with sacred trumpet

▼ Morris dancing in an English village street

▲ Musicians and sun-dancers from Peru, South America

▲ Christian procession in Andalusia, Spain, led by the town band

◄ Christian procession in Peru, led by the town trumpeter

More about
religious dancing B7, B16
religious music A16, B16, D5-7, E17, G13

▲ Dancing for the sisal harvest, Angola, Africa. Sisal is a kind of string

▶ Harvest procession in Britain 200 years ago

▲ Dancing for rain in Bulgaria 100 years ago

▶ Chinese New Year dance in Soho, London

> **More about**
> celebrations B12, D18

Music and the seasons

People use music to mark the seasons of the year. In Spring they sing planting-songs, as they plough the land and sow the seed. Summer and Autumn bring harvest-songs, as the produce is gathered and stored away. There are Winter songs, New Year songs, songs to sing on sunny days, and songs and dances for bringing rain. Work songs and holiday songs fill every month of the passing year.

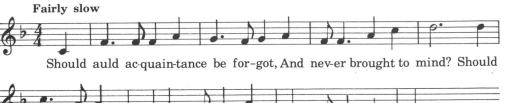

Should auld ac-quain-tance be for-got, And nev-er brought to mind? Should auld ac-quain-tance be for-got, And days o' lang — syne.

▲ *Auld Lang Syne*: sung in Britain and the USA on New Year's Eve

We use music in the seasons – the special occasions – of our lives, as well. There are songs and lullabies for babies, nursery rhymes and playground songs, music for weddings, birthdays and funerals. Whenever something important happens, we use music to make it special, to mark it out from ordinary, daily life.

Ring-a-ring o'ros-es, a pock-et full of po-sies, A-tish-oo! A-tish-oo! we all fall down.

▲ Some people say that *Ring-a-Ring o' Roses* was first made up about the plague, when many people fell down dead

Background music

When music is playing, what do you do? Do you concentrate on listening to it, or play it in the background while you get on with something else?

People often use the beat of background music to help in their work. Galley slaves, hundreds of years ago, used a steady drum-beat to keep the rowing together. Sailors sang sea shanties as they hauled on heavy ropes. Marching soldiers sang songs, or used a band, to keep in step. Many women today, in Africa or the East, sing work songs as their ancestors have done for thousands of years. Farmers planting rice, in the Far East and India, keep up a rhythm by singing songs.

▲ Minstrels playing for a feast in the Middle Ages; the instruments (left to right) are a fiddle, hurdy-gurdy, harp and psaltery

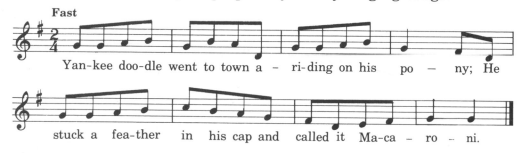

Yan-kee doo-dle went to town a – ri-ding on his po – ny; He stuck a fea-ther in his cap and called it Ma-ca – ro – ni.

▲ *Yankee Doodle* began as a soldiers' song in the American War of Independence, 1776

▼ African workers planting crops to the sound of xylophone, drum and a string instrument called a harp-lute

▲ Drum beats keep the galley slaves rowing together

▲ The cocoa harvest in Trinidad; people dance on the dried beans to polish them

Work-music is used in factories, too. In workshops and on production lines, cheerful music helps to drown the noise of machinery. It passes the time, and makes boring jobs more bearable. Background music is also used in shops, cafés and supermarkets. If it stopped, you would be surprised at the amount of noise you heard: clattering plates, private conversations, all kinds of rattles, bangs and shouts. Modern life is noisy, and background music helps to soften it. Some dentists even use music on their patients, to take their minds off everything else that is going on.

Folk music

In Europe and America nowadays, much of the music we hear has been specially 'composed'. That is, someone has made it up for other people to enjoy. We talk of 'Beethoven's Fifth Symphony', or 'The Blue Danube Waltz, by Johann Strauss' – the composer is as well known as the writer of a book.

But most of the world's music was not composed at all. It is called **folk music**, and it belongs to everyone. Often it is impossible to say who first made up each tune, or when. People learn folk music from each other, by heart. The same tunes are handed on for hundreds of years, and are sometimes changed as they travel from person to person and from place to place.

Every country in the world, every district, has its own folk tunes, and its own way of singing and playing them. Many are only known to local people. But others travel all over the world. Most North American and British people, for example, have played children's folk games like *Ring-a-Ring o' Roses,* or sung traditional songs like *Bobby Shaftoe* or *Greensleeves*. Most of us have seen or taken part in folk dancing (like American square dancing, Spanish flamenco, or Scottish reels).

Britain and America

Until 100 years ago, there were very few factories, very few industrial machines. In most places, the main occupations were farming and trade. Folk songs, too, were about country life: weather, crops, animals and birds, the loves and sorrows of ordinary people's lives. We still sing many of these songs today: for example, most people know *Barbara Allen* (about a hard-hearted lover), *John Brown's Body* (a marching song from the American Civil War), or nonsense-songs like *Old Macdonald had a Farm*.

▲ The muffin man, ringing and singing to attract customers. (The muffins are in the tray on his head)

▼ A masque or fancy-dress party in the 1600s. The musicians in the gallery are providing the music, just as a group might do today, and all the guests seem to be enjoying themselves

◄ Religious folk music: the Shakers, an American religious order, dance and sing hymns in 19th-century America

▼ 19th-century slaves in the Southern USA relax after a day's work, singing spirituals, playing the banjo and fiddle, and dancing

▲ 19th-century cowboys dance and play music in a saloon bar after the long trail driving the cattle west

When machines became common, and industrial towns grew, songs and ballads told about factories and industry. Many of them are still popular, for example *Comin' round the Mountain* (about the railways: the 'six white horses' are six puffs of white smoke), *The Gresford Disaster* (about a mine explosion in which 245 people died), and *Clementine* (a song from the 1849 gold rush in California).

Many folk songs have been used in church. Dozens of Christmas carols use folk tunes (for example *The Holly and the Ivy*). The tunes for hymns like *Morning has Broken* and *Immortal, Invisible God only Wise* also began life as folk tunes. **Spirituals** were songs sung by the slaves who worked in the American cotton fields of the 19th century; now they are sung all over the world. Famous ones include *I got a Robe, Swing low sweet Chariot*, and *Nobody knows the Trouble I've seen*.

Folk music in the 20th century

Towards the end of the 19th century, people became interested in collecting and preserving folk music. Collectors went round country districts with notebooks and (when they were invented) recording machines, asking people to sing and play for them. Books of folk music were published, and soon it was available everywhere, not just in its own local area. In school, for example, you will certainly hear, and perhaps sing and play, folk songs from a dozen different countries.

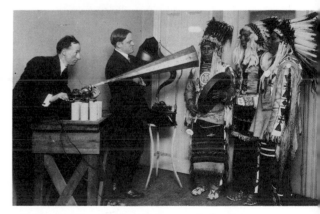

▲ Recording Indian folk music in the early days of the gramophone

◄ A folk group today; the instruments they are playing are (left to right) the banjo, three accordions, drums and a saxophone

More about
folk music B2-5, B8-16, D18, F24-25

Some folk music of the world

▼ Marching band (U.S.A.)

▼ Church choir (England)

▼ Bagpiper (Scotland)

▲ Country and western guitarist (U.S.A.)

▲ Limbo dancer (Jamaica)

▲ Flute players (Bolivia)

▲ Flamenco dancer and guitarist (Spain)

▲ Long drummers (Africa)

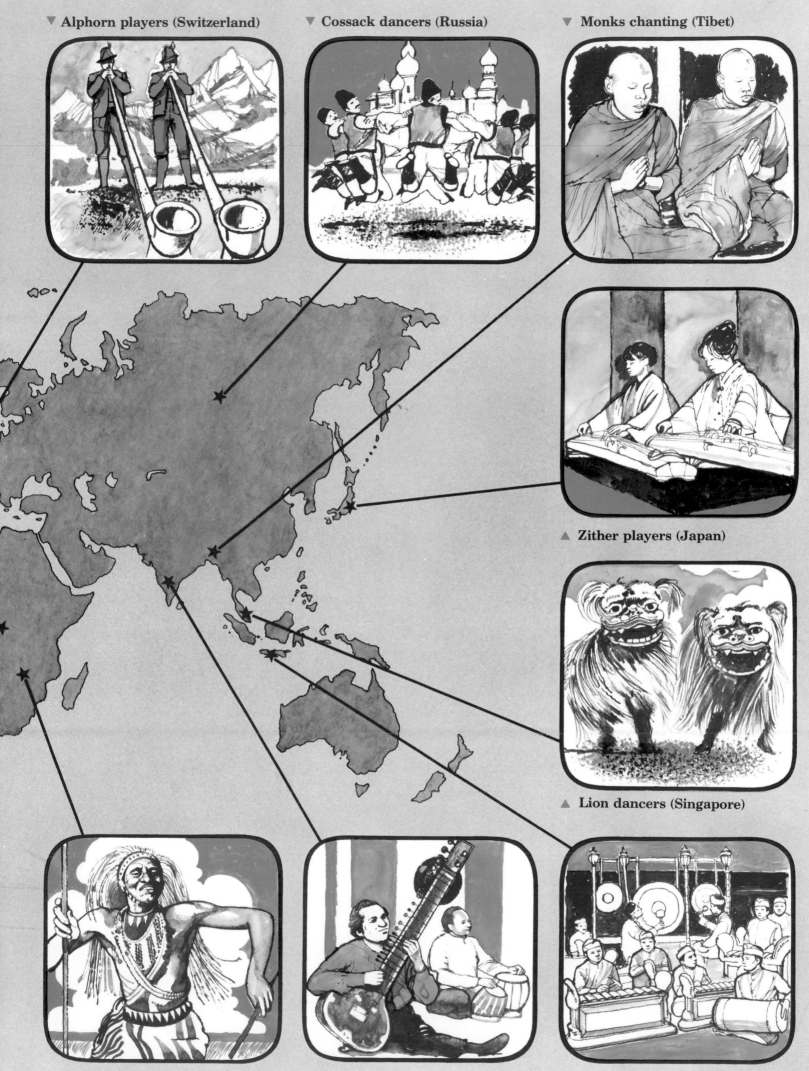

▼ Alphorn players (Switzerland)

▼ Cossack dancers (Russia)

▼ Monks chanting (Tibet)

▲ Zither players (Japan)

▲ Lion dancers (Singapore)

▲ Demon dancer (Africa)

▲ Sitar and tabla players (India)

▲ Gamelan orchestra (Java)

▲ Dancers and drummers from the Kudu tribe

▶ Dancers from the Tutsi tribe

▲ Nigerian musicians playing guitars made from gourds (dried fruit-skins)

▶ Kenyan musician with animal-horn

More about
folk music B2-9, B12-16, D18, F24-25
drums C15-16
West Indian music B12-13

African music

Modern Africa is developing fast. Modern cities, airports, and roads are changing the way in which many people live. If you travelled round African cities to find out what music people hear today, it would be the same kinds of pop and classical music as anywhere else in the modern world.

But Africa still has its folk music. Singing, dancing, and playing instruments are an important part of everyday life. People use music in religious ceremonies, for work, and for entertainment at weddings, birthdays, and parties.

Singing is very important in African music. Sometimes there is one single voice, sometimes a group of voices. Often two groups answer each other: they echo or repeat the music that has just been heard. The main instruments are pipes, curved trumpets and horns, wooden xylophones, and dozens of different shapes and sizes of drum. In many places, instruments are prized possessions. They are beautifully carved, and decorated with beads, polished shells, silver, and sometimes gold. Some people even treat them as though they were alive. They think that the instruments sleep in the instrument house, and wake up when they begin to play.

▲ Drums and balafon (a kind of xylophone) from the Bobo tribe

▼ These trumpets made from gourds are called hoo-hoos after the sound they make

▲ Harp player from Ethiopia

▼ Nigerian trumpet

The beat of African music is often fast, rhythmic, and full of complicated, ever-changing patterns. We are used to groups of 3 beats, or 4: African music also has groups of 5, 7, 11, and more – and mixes them together, too. Try tapping out groups of 4 beats, while a friend taps out groups of 5 at the same time. It is not easy, but it makes a lively sound. In African folk dancing, your feet might be following a 4-beat pattern, while your hips and arms were in 5. The different beats of the music are partly to help you keep them all together.

▼ Cymbal players from Morocco

Try tapping out these groups, first slowly, then getting faster. Make beat 1 heavier than the rest. How long can you keep together?

You	1 2 3 4 1 2 3 4 1 2 3 4 1 2 3 4 1 2 3 4 etc.
Friend	1 2 3 4 5 1 2 3 4 5 1 2 3 4 5 1 2 3 4 5 etc.

West Indian music

▲ Steel band music at the Port of Spain Carnival, Trinidad

▶ The Jamaican folk song *Hill an' Gully*. A gully is a dip in the land between two hills

In 1492 the explorer Christopher Columbus set out to find a new way of reaching India, by sailing West instead of East. He never did reach India; but he came to some undiscovered islands in the Caribbean Sea, and called them the West Indies. The West Indies had rich, fertile soil, and lush vegetation. They were ideal for growing huge quantities of crops like bananas and sugar-cane. The owners built vast plantations over the islands, and to work them they imported thousands of slaves from Africa. The slaves brought African music and African stories with them. So West Indian music began. At first it was African, but as the years passed it grew more and more separate, until by the time the slaves were set free (in the middle of the 19th century), it had sounds and a special style all of its own.

Many of the folk songs of the West Indies come from the days of slavery. The beautiful Jamaican folk song, *Day oh Day oh*, was first sung by women slaves as they loaded bananas into the waiting ships. Have you heard *Hill an' Gully*? It began as a work song for men digging ditches to bring water to the fields. The singing kept the rhythm of their pickaxes smooth.

In Trinidad, a favourite form of music was (and still is) the **calypso**. Calypsos began as protest songs, full of the harsh life of the slaves on the big sugar plantations. Calypso is now the main music of Carnival (30 days of song, processions and feasting in February, before the self-denying days of Lent begin). Many calypsos have funny or mocking words; their rhythm and the sound of the steel bands who play them have carried them round the world. At carnival time in Port of Spain, the capital of Trinidad, the steel bands playing calypsos as they dance through the streets can have as many as 1000 musicians.

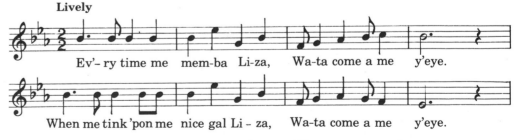

▲ Another musician from Trinidad. He is playing a guiro, a kind of scraper

▲ One of the most famous Jamaican calypsos, *Wata come a me y'eye*

▶ A Jamaican limbo dancer

◀ Slaves working a treadmill (to provide power for a factory)

▼ Bob Marley, the king of reggae music, who died in 1981

The West Indies took slaves from many parts of Africa. There were dozens of different religions, Moslem, Hindu, pagan and Christian. Each religion had its own music, its own distinctive sound. Some have grown into new, West Indian sounds. One of the best of these is **reggae**. At first it was the music of a religious, political group. But now it is known world-wide, as an important branch of pop.

Steel bands

Steel bands first became popular in the 1940s, in Trinidad. They soon spread to other parts of the Caribbean, and now they are well known in many countries. They play pop, classical and dance music, and of course calypsos.

Steel bands use drums in several sizes, tuned to play different notes. At first drums were roughly made: steel oil-drums (left by American soldiers after the 1939–45 war, or left over from the West Indian oil industry) whose tops were hammered into shape. Nowadays drums (or **pans** as they are called) are made by special pan-makers.

There are three main sizes of pan. The **ping pong** (called after its sound) is the smallest, and plays the highest notes. In the band, the ping pong pans usually play the tune. The middle drum is called **second pan** or **guitar pan.** It has lower notes than the ping pong, and usually plays the accompaniment. The **cello pans** and **bass pans** play the lowest notes. There is also the **rhythm section** (drums, maracas, cymbals, guiro etc.) to give the beat.

▼ The pans in a steel band

BASS

GUITARS AND DOUBLE SECONDS

CELLOS

PING PONGS

RHYTHM SECTION

▲ Testing a steel drum. Each note is tapped to make sure it is in tune

More about
bands B30-32
drums C15-16
African music B10-11

A snake-charmer playing a wind instrument called a pungi

Indian music

Pop music

Musical films are very popular in India. Hundreds are made and shown every year, far more than in any other country in the world. The films are full of songs sung by Indian pop stars. Hit songs from the films are sold on records, too, and played over pop stations on the radio. Sometimes hit songs from America or Europe are translated into Indian languages, and performed with Indian instruments and an Indian singing style.

Classical music

Indian classical music is quite unlike the classical music we know in the West (for example, Beethoven symphonies or Tchaikovsky concertos). It is not written down, but learned by heart, and passed on from teacher to pupil. The players start each piece with a basic pattern of notes and a basic rhythm, and alter and adapt them as they play. This is called *improvising*, and it makes each performance completely new, different from all the others. (The same idea is used in jazz: you can read about it on page B22.)

The basic note-group is called a **raga** (pronounced RAH-ga, or sometimes just RAHG). Ragas are like short tunes of five, six, or seven notes. Each raga is connected with a different season, or time of day. (There is a 'rain' raga, for example, and there are 'sunrise' and 'sunset' ragas too.) Each raga has its own mood (joyful, dreamy, sorrowful, and so on). When you improvise, you keep repeating the note-pattern of the raga, adapting it as you go along.

Trumpeters and folk-dancers in the Himalayas

Rag bhairav — Drone notes

An Indian painting of musicians and dancing-girls performing at the wedding of a 16th-century Emperor

▲ This is an early morning raga: dreamy and peaceful, like wisps of cloud parting to reveal the sun. The drone notes are played all through the piece, first one and then the other

The basic rhythmic group is called a **tala** (pronounced TAH-la, or sometimes just TAHL). Each tala is built up like a chain, and each link in the chain has the same beats as all the others. The links often have special meanings. Two long notes linked by one short note, for example (o o o , DAH-da-DAH), mean 'elephant'. Just as you base the *notes* of your performance on a raga, so you base the *rhythms* on a tala, varying it as you go along.

10-beat tala

You	1 2 3 4 5 6 7 8 9 10	1 2 3 4 5 6 7 8 9 10
A friend	(clap)	(clap) (clap) (clap)

▲ This needs two people. You count or tap equal beats. Your friend claps hands where the arrows come. Repeat the whole tala as many times as you like, but end on beat 1 (not on beat 10), with a final clap. This tala is called *Japtal*

More about improvising B22, G10

Music of the Far East

Like Indian music, Far Eastern music uses quite different rhythms and scales from those of the West. One of the simplest and best known is the five-note, or **pentatonic** scale. (Play five of the black notes on a piano, in order, up or down, and ask a friend what country comes to mind.)

Entertainment music

In the past, ordinary people enjoyed music played by travelling musicians in village streets, fields, or inns. Rich noblemen were fond of dances, songs, and drama. The dancers were often acrobats as well. They performed to the music of singers, while a small band played. In the drama, actors performed a story in silent, mime movements, while the words and music were provided by musicians at one side of the stage.

You can enjoy all these kinds of music today. On the islands of Bali and Java, for example, you can watch dancers performing to the sound of a **gamelan** (GAM-e-lan) orchestra (drums, gongs, rattles, and several different sizes of xylophone). In Japan, you can watch actors in **Noh** plays (based on religious themes), or **Kabuki** (ka-BOO-kee) plays which tell stories of ordinary life, in dance. Also in Japan, **Geisha** (GAY-sha) girls will sing and play to entertain you. Korean and Malaysian dancers often visit the West, and give us a glimpse of the richness and colour of their country's music.

▲ Dancers from Bangkok, Thailand, performing a traditional dance

◄ Singers in a Japanese opera

▼ Gamelan orchestra from Java with xylophones and chimes

▲ Barong dance with gamelan orchestra on the island of Bali

◄ A beautiful old silk painting of a Japanese Geisha orchestra

▲ People thought that when he played his lute (a guitar-like instrument), this powerful Chinese king could control the elements of earth, air, fire and water

Temple music

Music has always been important in Far Eastern religion. Sometimes the priests and monks chant prayers. At other times the worshippers sit silently, in *meditation*. While they do this, a plucked instrument is played. The words of prayers are carved on tiny handbells, or on strips of metal to hang in trees, and in the temple eaves. Then, when the wind blows or the bells are rung, the prayers are set free to sound in the ears of God.

Dancing is part of many Far Eastern temple ceremonies. The dancers join the dance-group as children of six or seven, and train for many years. The women's dancing includes skilful movements of tiny muscles (eyebrows, cheeks, finger-joints) as well as of arms, body and legs. Some of the men's dances are like plays, with warrior-gods fighting fearsome demons. The demons are made of cloth over wooden frames, and carried by several dancers hiding underneath. The dancing is accompanied by singing, and by the music of flutes, gongs, xylophones and drums.

▶ Japanese flute player

▶ Dancers from Singapore in lion costume

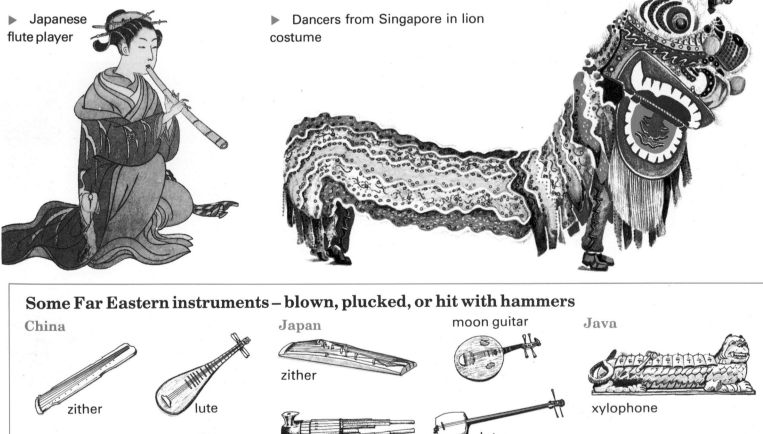

Some Far Eastern instruments – blown, plucked, or hit with hammers

China

zither

lute

flute

gong

Japan

zither

bamboo mouth organ

moon guitar

lute

Java

xylophone

Bali

gamelan orchestra, played with hammers of wood or metal

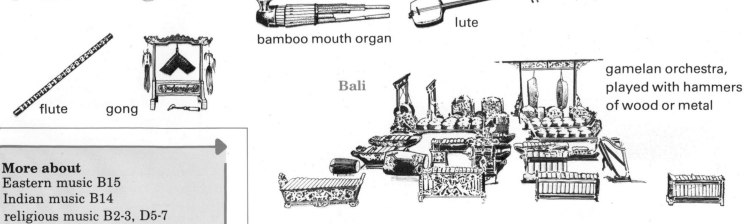

More about
Eastern music B15
Indian music B14
religious music B2-3, D5-7

Entertainers past and present

There have been skilled entertainers since music began. In early times, anyone in a tribe who could sing or dance particularly well was admired, and had a special job to do, performing at festivals and feasts. Sometimes he was a priest or a medicine-man as well, and the tribesmen thought his music one of his magic powers.

All over the world, **bards** used to be popular. A bard's job was to tell people stories, often singing or chanting them to musical accompaniment. In the days when few people knew how to read, and before radio or television were invented, the village bard was an important man. Have you heard any of the hero-stories of Ancient Greece, the Anansi stories of Africa and Trinidad, or the Brer Rabbit stories of the southern United States? Those are the kind of folk tales that bards performed.

In the castles and towns of the Middle Ages, professional entertainers called **troubadours** (troo-ba-DOORS) and **minstrels** sang songs and played instruments, and **tumblers** played instruments, danced, and did acrobatic tricks. Today you can sometimes see a **busker** in the street: someone who plays, dances, or sings, while passers-by leave him coins to pay for his music.

▲ A medieval bard singing at a feast, accompanied by a harpist

▲ Entertainment in the Middle Ages. A drummer and piper play while an acrobat performs a difficult trick with swords

▲ Victorian buskers playing to a group of children

▼ Modern troubadours playing folk music in Hanover, Germany

▶ A one-man band

> **More about**
> entertainers of the past B18, E6, E10-11, E14-15, E18-19, E20-21, E27, E29
> of the East B15
> popular singers B20-21, B24-27

Music in the theatre

In the theatre, music has always been popular. In Shakespeare's time, actors shared their theatres with jugglers, performing animals (like dancing bears), dancers, and singers. Often a play ended with singing and dancing, or had musical interludes, breaks in the middle of the story while people danced, played, or sang.

In 19th-century Europe, a favourite evening entertainment was the **song-room** or **supper-room**. Here people sat at tables, eating and drinking, while on a stage at one end of the room entertainers performed, and musicians played and sang popular songs. Often the audience joined in. This idea developed into modern night-clubs, working-men's clubs, and cabaret (CAB-ar-ay). In all of these, the customers can eat, drink, and sometimes dance, as well as watch the show. Song-rooms also developed into the **music-hall**. In a music-hall the customers could still eat and drink, but they sat in rows, like a theatre audience. The entertainment was mainly songs, but might also include dancers, jugglers, and comedians. 100 years ago, people in towns used to visit the music-hall (or **vaudeville**, VAW-de-vil, as it was sometimes called), as we go to the cinema today.

Proper theatres were larger than music-halls, and could put on bigger, more spectacular shows. In the theatre today, you can enjoy all kinds of different musical entertainments, from pop concerts and rock operas to opera, ballet, and pantomime.

When films, radio, and television were invented, they offered people the same kinds of entertainment as theatre, cabaret, or music-hall. Nowadays, if you want to see a pantomime, concert, variety show or musical, you can go out to the theatre or cinema – or you can watch in comfort in your own home.

▲ A musician playing for acrobats, a tight-rope walker and a performing monkey in Shakespeare's time

▼ The cover of a book of music-hall songs with pictures of the favourite music-halls in 19th-century London

◄ Cartoon showing minstrels from a 19th-century American vaudeville show

▼ Cowboy variety show in 19th-century Wyoming, USA

▲ Modern pantomime: a scene from
Toad of Toad Hall

▲ 19th-century pantomime in Drury
Lane Theatre, London

Musical shows

Variety show

The programme consists of 'acts': dancers, singers, comedians, and sometimes jugglers or acrobats. A band plays music to accompany the acts, and the costumes and stage settings are often lavish and colourful.

Pantomime

Pantomimes are normally put on at Christmas and New Year. A pantomime is a fairy-tale (like *Cinderella* or *Aladdin*) told as a kind of musical play. Pantomimes are full of songs and dancing, and sometimes include jugglers or even performing animals. The story always has a handsome hero, a beautiful heroine, a wicked villain, and a comic 'dame' (an ugly old woman, usually acted by a man). There is often a chorus of singers and dancers in colourful costumes, and the music is provided by the theatre band. Some pantomimes nowadays are performed on ice, and all the performers move about on skates.

Musical

Musicals are a modern form of an older entertainment called 'operetta' or 'light opera'. The story is told in a play full of songs and dancing. The songs often become hits on their own, quite separate from the rest of the show. Some of the best musicals of this century are also films. For example, the 'dance musicals' starring Fred Astaire or Gene Kelly, and the musicals written by Rodgers and Hammerstein (such as *The King and I, Oklahoma, The Sound of Music*) are often shown in cinemas and on television. More recent musicals include *Oliver!* and *West Side Story*.

Rock opera

Rock operas are like musicals, but use rock music. Some of the best known are *Godspell* and *Joseph and the Amazing Technicolor Dreamcoat*. Like musicals, rock operas can be full of hit songs, and are often popular as films as well as on the stage.

Opera and ballet

You can read more about these in Section D, *Singing and Dancing*.

▲ The musical *Oliver*: the scene where
Oliver Twist asks for more gruel

More about
music in Shakespeare's time
  E14-15
19th-century music E22-23,
  E26-27
musical films B27, D23-25

B19

Popular singers

Hits of the past

All through the history of music, some tunes have been hits as soon as they first appeared. For some, success is short, a few weeks or months. But for others it can last long after the time when they first appeared. In the time of Queen Elizabeth I, for example, a favourite song was *Greensleeves* – and millions of people, all round the world, know it still.

Fairly slowly

A – las, my love, you do me wrong to cast me off__ dis-court-eous-ly; and

I have lov – ed you so long, de – light-ing in __ your com-pan-y.

▲ Elizabethan lute player

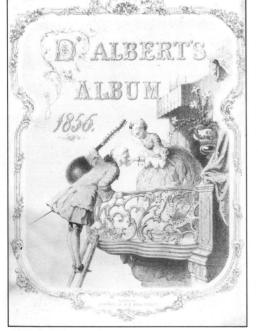

▲ Three covers of some popular sheet music of Victorian times

▶ *Daisy Bell*, a favourite music-hall song

Waltz time

Dai — sy, Dai — sy, Give me your an-swer, do! ____

I'm half cra — zy, All for the love of you! ____

What is a hit?

The word 'hit' comes from the tournaments of medieval knights. It is connected with jousting (that is, when two knights gallop towards each other in full armour, each trying to knock the other off his horse). If your lance struck your opponent's armour hard enough to break the fragile tip, that was called a 'hit'. In the music business, a hit is a tune that everyone seems to like, buy, and remember almost as soon as it is published. For your record to be a hit nowadays (and to go into the 'charts', the list of the week's best sellers), it must sell at least 100,000 copies.

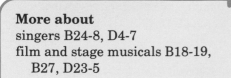

More about
singers B24-8, D4-7
film and stage musicals B18-19, B27, D23-5

Silent films and 'talkies'

One of the most striking moments in the history of popular music was the showing of *The Jazz Singer* in 1927. *The Jazz Singer* was the first-ever talking and singing film (called a 'talkie'). Until then, people were used to silent acting in films, accompanied by a piano or orchestra actually in the cinema. But when Al Jolson, the star of *The Jazz Singer*, opened his mouth to sing, his voice seemed to come from the screen. The audience was amazed; someone even ran round behind the screen, to see if Jolson and his orchestra were hiding there.

Crooners

Al Jolson was famous for a romantic, sentimental kind of song: you may have heard *Mammy*, or *Swannee*, or *Sonny Boy*. Later, a husky, throaty kind of singing called 'crooning' became popular. The most famous crooner of all was Bing Crosby. Because of the way he sang, people nicknamed him 'The Old Groaner'. This kind of music is still one of the commonest today. As well as to Bing Crosby, listen to Frank Sinatra, or to Ella Fitzgerald.

Some hit tunes of the past

How many do you know?

Middle Ages	*Sumer is icumen in; The Coventry Carol; Agincourt Song*
1500–1600	*Greensleeves*
1600–1700	*Portsmouth*
1700–1800	*Rule, Britannia; Drink to Me only; Yankee Doodle*
1800–1900	*The Old Folks at Home; Lily of Laguna; After the Ball; Beautiful Dreamer; My Grandfather's Clock*
1900–1910	*Maple Leaf Rag*
1910–1920	*Alexander's Ragtime Band; Pack up your Troubles*
1920–1930	*Tea For Two; Black Bottom; Old Man River*
1930–1940	*Brother, Can You spare a Dime?; The Lady is a Tramp*
1940–1950	*You'll never walk alone; White Christmas*
1950–1960	*Rock around the Clock; Heartbreak Hotel; Living Doll*
1960–1970	*I want to hold your Hand; Blowin' in the Wind; Puppet on a String; I can't get no Satisfaction*
1970–1980	*Rivers of Babylon; Mull of Kintyre*
1980–	*Brick in the Wall; Japanese Boy*

▲ Frank Sinatra, Bing Crosby, and Ella Fitzgerald

Jazz

Jazz began towards the end of the 19th century, in the Southern States of the USA. It was music of black people who had once been slaves. It was a mixture of their hymns, work songs, and spirituals. The way of singing, and the rhythmic beat, came partly from the African folk music brought to America by the slaves' ancestors. Ideas were also taken from popular music of the time, especially music-hall songs, and from a kind of jerky, rhythmic piano music called **ragtime**.

One of the main ideas of jazz, right from those early days, was **improvising**. While one instrument (often trumpet) played the tune, another (often clarinet) played faster notes, decorations, and new melodies round it. The player made up these decorations on the spot, and the art of making them up is called 'improvising'. (It is rather like the improvising used in Indian classical music.) Improvising is one of the main parts of a jazz musician's skill.

Jazz first became popular outside the Southern States in the 1910s and 1920s. Jazz bands began making records, and these spread the sound all over America and Europe. Many popular songs (like *When the Saints go marchin' in*) and dances (like the *Charleston* and *Black Bottom*) used jazz ideas, and jazz musicians (like Louis Armstrong, or Jelly Roll Morton and his band, called the Red Hot Peppers) played or improvised round popular tunes.

▲ The jazz trumpeter Miles Davis

▼ *When the Saints go marchin' in*. The saints are marching into heaven, following Jesus

March time

Oh when the saints _____ go march-in' in, _____ oh when the saints go march-in' in, _____ I wan-na be there in that num-ber, _____ when the saints go march-in' in.

▼ The saxophone, an important jazz instrument, comes in several sizes. Here you can see, from left to right, tenor, alto and soprano

As well as players, there have been many fine jazz singers. They often sing songs of a special sort called **The Blues**. Blues songs have sad words, and a dragging, sliding kind of tune. (If you want to hear Blues singing at its best, try records by Bessie Smith or Billie Holliday.)

All through the 20th century, jazz has continued to grow and change. Nowadays the two most important kinds are called **traditional jazz** (which is mainly fast songs and slow blues), and **modern jazz** (which uses ideas and instruments from classical and Eastern music, blended with the original American style).

The instruments of jazz

A jazz band usually consists of about four to ten players. The basis is always the **rhythm section**, which provides the beat of the music. There is a drummer, a bass player (usually a double bass, but sometimes a bass electric guitar), and a harmony instrument (usually piano, banjo or guitar). On top of this the **melody instruments** are added. In traditional jazz bands they are clarinet, trumpet, and trombone. Modern jazz often uses other instruments, for example saxophone, vibraphone, violin, or flute.

Swing bands

As well as small jazz bands, larger groups in the 1920s–1950s also played jazz, especially for dancing and for records. They were called swing bands (because their music had a 'swinging' rhythm), and some were as popular then as pop groups are today. Some big bands played mainly jazz, for listening: two of the most famous were the bands led by Duke Ellington and Count Basie. Other bands played for dancing: two of the most popular were led by Paul Whiteman and Glenn Miller. Swing bands often had their own solo singers: Bing Crosby and Frank Sinatra, for example, began their careers singing with particular bands.

The instruments in a swing band (16–60 players) were arranged in three main sections: **rhythm** (drums, piano, guitar, and bass), **wind** (mainly saxophones), and **brass** (mainly trumpets and trombones). A few bands used **strings** (violins, violas and cellos) as well.

▲ Jazz band on a Mississippi river-boat in 1918. The trumpet player nearest the piano is Louis Armstrong. How many of the instruments can you name?

▲ Count Basie, the king of big band jazz

Some famous jazz performers

There are many different kinds of jazz, and it is hard to suggest records that everyone is bound to like. The performers in this list have made LP collections of their greatest hits. If you have never heard any jazz before at all, try records by the starred names first.

* Original Dixieland Jazz Band (one of the first 'traditional' bands)
  Louis Armstrong (trumpeter and singer)
  Bessie Smith (Blues singer)
  Duke Ellington and his Orchestra
* Benny Goodman and his Band
* Billie Holliday (singer)
  Charlie Parker (saxophone player)
  Art Tatum (piano player)
  Modern Jazz Quartet (one of the first 'modern jazz' groups)
  Stephane Grappelli (violin player)
  Miles Davis (trumpet player)
* Oscar Peterson (piano player)

More about
African music B10-11
bands B12-13, B30-2
drums C15-16
improvising B14, G10

Pop

Rock 'n' roll

Modern pop music started in 1954, when a record called *Shake, rattle and roll* became a best-seller in the USA and in Europe, almost overnight. It was made by a group called Bill Haley and the Comets, and the kind of music was something completely new. It was called **rock 'n' roll**. A few weeks later, Bill Haley had another hit, *Rock around the Clock,* and modern pop was here to stay.

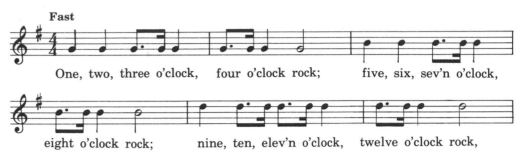

Fast

One, two, three o'clock,   four o'clock rock;   five, six, sev'n o'clock,

eight o'clock rock;   nine, ten, elev'n o'clock,   twelve o'clock rock,

▲ Bill Haley and the Comets

▼ Elvis Presley (he was nicknamed 'Elvis the Pelvis' for wriggling his hips in time to the music)

▲ Bill Haley's second hit *Rock around the Clock*

At first, the music was intended for dancing. (If you didn't want to get up and dance, you could do **hand jive** in your chair. You can see some of the hand jive movements in the box on this page.) The beat was the most important thing – a pulsing, throbbing rhythm that pushed the music and the dancing along. Soon, however, people wanted something more interesting to listen to. Rock 'n' roll singers like Elvis Presley, Buddy Holly and the Everly Brothers made records that had something to say as well as a pounding beat.

▼ Some of Elvis Presley's million-or-more-selling hit singles

Some hand jive movements

Do all of these sitting down. Keep to the order of movements in each box. You can do the boxes in any order, and as often as you like.

A Count 1-2   Count 3-4

Slap right hand down on right thigh, and at the same time left hand on left thigh, *twice*. Hold your bent left elbow in your right hand, and draw a small circle in the air with the first finger of your left hand, *twice*.

B Count 1-2   Count 3-4

(Same slaps as in A.) Hold your bent right elbow in your left hand, and draw a small circle in the air with the first finger of your right hand, *twice*.

C Count 1-2   Count 3-4

Hold your hands out in front of you, with the fingers stretched and stiff. Wag your right hand above your left hand, *twice*. Then move your left hand above your right, *twice*.

D Count 1-2   Count 3-4

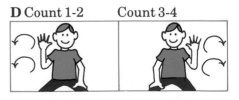

Hold up your open right hand, like a policeman stopping traffic. Move it in a small circle, as if you were cleaning a window, *twice*. Then do the same with your left hand, *twice*.

◀ The Rolling Stones

▼ The Supremes

Rhythm and blues

The beat, and the way of singing rock 'n' roll, grew out of an earlier kind of music called **rhythm and blues**. As its name says, this was a mixture of sharp jazz rhythms and the sliding, 'edgy' sound of the Blues. Whatever the sound they use, almost all pop performers base their music on the beat and sound of rhythm and blues. It can lead, for example, to the brassy, jazzy Tamla Motown sound of Diana Ross and the Supremes or The Temptations, to the gentler surfin' sound of The Beach Boys, or to the wild, driving music of The Rolling Stones and The Who.

The Beatles

One of the greatest groups in the story of pop is The Beatles. They came together as professionals in 1959, and their first hit record, *Please please me*, came out in 1962. They continued to work together until 1970, when each went his own way. Why are they important? Simply because, at a time when a fair amount of pop was forgotten almost as soon as it was performed, they made pop music *musical*. They took time over each record, and were never satisfied to go on producing the same sound just because it made a hit. Their music was crammed with new ideas, and had ideas in it that no one in pop had used before.

▲ Ticket-stubs for a Beatles concert in 1964

▲ Official letter-heading used on notepaper for the Beatles Fan Club

◀ The Beatles in concert at the start of their fame

▲ Pop concert – performers and audience

▲ Pop concert – behind the scenes

▼ Rod Stewart in concert

Pop music now

In the 1970s, pop developed in many different ways. In particular, the new uses musicians found for loudspeakers, amplifiers, and electronic instruments helped to make the electronics industry one of the most adventurous and fastest-growing of the century.

1970s pop groups often played music very far from the original, driving sound of rock 'n' roll. There was **soul music** (which adds the sound of American gospel songs); **folk rock** (using styles and ideas from the folk music of the American Middle West); **teenybopper** or **bubblegum music** (with an easy, rhythmic style); **middle-of-the-road** pop (like the music of Abba or Elton John); and **punk** (protest music, often aiming for a violent, ugly sound). For some listeners, the most exciting pop of all is progressive music, meant for listening rather than for dancing. It is normally called **rock** (sometimes **hard rock** or **heavy rock**), and it includes the work of some of the most famous performers in the history of pop: Pink Floyd, Jethro Tull, Yes, Led Zeppelin, and Genesis. During the late 1970s and the early 1980s **reggae** became popular. Reggae started in the West Indies with Jamaican sounds and ideas as well as a basic style of rhythm and blues. Progressive rock also remained popular in the early 1980s, using new instruments and styles. Sometimes it was close to classical music, too. And performers like Mike Oldfield and Emerson, Lake and Palmer worked with classical soloists and orchestras. Other musicians who have influenced pop music in the 1980s are Kate Bush and The Police.

▼ The Who in concert

Whose records to listen to

There are thousands of different singers and groups. The ones named here are among the most important in the story of pop. Try, first, records by names in **heavy type**. (If the name of your favourite group is missing – sorry! There was simply no room to put in everyone.)

ROCK 'N' ROLL
Bill Haley, Elvis Presley, Chuck Berry, Jerry Lee Lewis

RHYTHM AND BLUES
Muddy Waters, Bo Diddley, **The Rolling Stones**

FOLK ROCK
The Byrds, Simon and Garfunkel

REGGAE
Bob Marley and the Wailers, Third World

SOUL MUSIC
Ray Charles, The Three Degrees, The Stylistics

ROCK
Cream, **Led Zeppelin,** David Bowie, **T Rex, Wings**

MAINSTREAM
The Carpenters, **Abba, Rod Stewart,** Elton John

OTHERS
Tamla Motown: **Stevie Wonder, Diana Ross, The Supremes**
Surf music: The Beach Boys
Teenybopper: **The Bay City Rollers,** The Jackson Five
Reggae: **Bob Marley and the Wailers**
Progressive: The Grateful Dead, Genesis, **Mike Oldfield**
Punk: Patti Smith, The Sex Pistols

▶ Some pop stars to listen for: Elvis Presley, Diana Ross, Stevie Wonder, Rod Stewart, Marc Bolan (and T Rex), Roger Daltrey (and The Who)

Some well known 'pop' films

See them if you get the chance!

Rock around the Clock (1956). The first pop film. When it was shown, rock 'n' roll was the latest news. Teenagers danced in the cinemas, and ripped up the seats. There were protests, and people tried to have the film banned. Does it still seem so shocking nowadays?

Jailhouse Rock (1958). One of the most enjoyable of Elvis Presley's films. He plays a convict who becomes a pop star. The music is some of Presley's best.

A Hard Day's Night (1964). A funny film by The Beatles, about the hard life a pop group leads, always travelling, always besieged by fans.

Yellow Submarine (1968). In this full length cartoon, The Beatles drive the nasty Blue Meanies away, and save Pepperland for all who love music. The songs are from one of the Beatles' best LPs, *Sergeant Pepper's Lonely Hearts' Club Band*.

▲ A poster for the Beatles' film *Yellow Submarine*

Woodstock (1969). A film about one of the most famous pop festivals ever held. Marvellous music from The Who, Jimi Hendrix, and Crosby Stills Nash and Young.

Saturday Night Fever (1977). A rather silly story, but full of magnificent disco dancing by John Travolta.

More about
films B19, B21, D23-5
pop music B24-6
electronic instruments C22
records B28-9

Records and recording

For thousands of years, right up to the year 1877, musicians worked and earned their living in much the same ways. All music-making was live: that is, the audience sat and listened while real, live performers played. That meant, of course, that if you wanted to hear a particular performer, you had to wait till he came to you, or you had to go to him. The composer Bach, for example, as a boy, once decided to go and hear the playing of an organist called Reinken. Bach lived in Lüneberg, and Reinken in Hamburg, 48 kilometres away. Bach walked all the way, there and back.

Nowadays, people still make this kind of journey to hear their favourite performers – by bus or train, not on foot. But it is easier to listen to your favourite music at home. We can do this because of what happened in 1877. That was the year when Thomas Edison, an American inventor, made the first-ever **recording machine**.

There had been a few machines to make music before: mechanical organs, musical boxes, even clockwork zithers and violins. But none of them used real performances by real people. With the **phonograph** (or 'sound-writer', as Edison called his machine), you could record a living person, and hear him or her give the same performance again and again. (We can still hear Edison himself, for example, many years after his death. Soon after inventing the phonograph, he made a recording to show how well it worked. What did he record? 'Mary had a little lamb . . . ')

Even though the first records were scratchy and fuzzy, they soon became popular, and by 1900 famous 'artists' (singers and players) had begun to think of making records as part of their job. The performer makes the record only once: then, every time a copy is sold, he is paid a **royalty** (usually about one twentieth of the record's price). For many performers today, record royalties are the main part of their income, earning more than their live performances.

The first well known record stars were opera singers of the early 1900s. The most famous was the tenor Caruso: He made 154 records (a huge number for those days), and his name was known, mainly from his records, all over the world.

But the best-selling recorded music of all was (and still is) jazz, popular songs, and pop. One singer, Bing Crosby, sold over 400 million records between 1927 and 1977: this was the largest number sold by any single artist since recording began. The best-selling group is The Beatles, with (so far) a staggering 600 million 'singles' and over 100 million LPs.

▲ A family listening to Edison's phonograph

▲ One of the first gramophones to play flat records. Earlier ones, like the others on this page, used wax cylinders

▲ In the early days of recording, the player had to stand very close to the gramophone

▶ Getting the piano ready for a recording session today

◀ Recording an orchestra at the beginning of the century. The master disc is in the machine in the front of the picture. Below you can see how records are made today

More about
Bach F2-3
Beatles B25, B27
Crosby B21
recording sessions C27

members of group each in own soundproofed booth

control room

backup orchestra

soloist

rest room

editing the tape

cutting grooves in an aluminium master

coating the master ready for the stamper

record press stamping out the discs

putting the finished discs into their sleeves

Bands

What is a band?

The word 'band', in music, was once used to mean a group of musicians who normally played in the open air. They often marched as they played, so they avoided instruments too heavy or bulky to carry (like organs or harpsichords). They left quiet instruments (like violins or guitars) for indoor use, and used instead instruments whose sound would carry well: brass instruments (such as trumpets and horns), woodwind instruments (such as high-pitched pipes and flutes), and percussion instruments (such as cymbals and drums).

Nowadays, most bands play inside as well as out of doors. We use the word 'band' for several kinds of groups: **military bands, brass bands**, and bands who play for entertainment (for example jazz bands, steel bands, theatre bands, and pop bands).

Military bands

Since earliest times, wherever there have been armies, there have been bands. Pictures of soldiers marching into battle 3000 years ago show musicians with trumpets and horns. (You can see what they looked like, from the picture on this page.)

In battle, music had several jobs to do. It was used for signalling orders (because a trumpet-call or drum-roll carried much further, over the noise of the fighting, than a shout or call). It was used to keep the soldiers in line, to help them march in step. Its stirring sounds kept your own side's spirits up – and impressed or terrified your enemies.

▲ A Turkish military band from ancient times

▶ An Iron Age army setting out for battle. The band (in the bottom right-hand corner) are playing long war trumpets with dragon heads

▼ This famous picture shows a fife player and drummers celebrating American Independence, 1776

Pipe band

This is a kind of military band that consists of **bagpipes** and **drums**. Nowadays we usually think of Scottish pipers with kilts and tartans. But other countries have bagpipes too. The sound of bagpipes carries particularly well in the open air.

▶ Piper of the Scots Guards in full-dress uniform playing the bagpipes

A modern military band, leading the Republic Day Parade in Delhi, India

(There is a story of Roman soldiers, invading Britain in 43 AD. As they started to leave their ships, they heard an unearthly wailing sound from behind the British waiting on the shore. Thinking it came from ghosts, they were about to turn and run – until their general showed them it was a bagpipe band, hidden behind a sand dune. If he had not noticed that, the Romans might have fled from the battle and sailed for home.)

When the fighting was done, the band had other jobs to do. It was used to play for funerals and to honour the dead. (You may have heard the *Last Post* played by trumpeters on Remembrance Day.) It was used for recruiting: a group of soldiers went round towns and villages, and the band played cheerful music to attract a crowd. Then the soldiers tried to persuade people to join the army, and go to war. Most important of all, the band played on ceremonial occasions, for parades and displays of every kind.

Nowadays, there is no place for a band on the battlefield. Modern war is too fast (because of planes and tanks) and too noisy (because of bombs and heavy guns). Signals are given by radio: there is no need for trumpet-calls. So military bands, today, are always used for show. They appear on great occasions like Mayday Parades, or at stations and airports to welcome visiting Heads of State. Their marching, and their music, are vital parts of ceremonies like Trooping the Colour in Britain, or the Liberty Parade in the USA.

The instruments of a military band

There are no fixed rules about which instruments must be used in a military band. Most bands include *clarinets* (1), *cornets* (6), *trombones* (5) and *euphoniums* of different sizes. Some add *piccolos* (3), *bassoons* (9), *horns* (4) and *marching tubas* (2). *Drums* (8), *cymbals* (7), and other percussion instruments (even portable *xylophones*) are common. The bass drummer gives a loud, clear beat which helps to keep the band in step.

▶ Salvation Army Band playing in a London street

▼ A brass band in a New York street, 100 years ago

▲ Dodge City Cowboy Band, Kansas City, USA, in 1882

▶ American school marching band in a Memorial Day parade

More about
brass band instruments C7-10
military band instruments
C4-10, C16

Brass bands

At the beginning of the 19th century, ordinary people started playing in brass bands for fun. Factory workers and miners often formed bands; the factory owner provided the instruments, and the bandsmen practised in their spare time when their day's work was done. There was always fierce loyalty to the local band. In some places, people supported their bands as keenly as we support football or baseball teams today.

The instruments in a brass band are brass and percussion. (Sometimes the instruments are silver-plated, and the band may be called a 'Silver Band'; but the actual instruments are the same.) Bands vary in size, from very small (four or five players) to large (40 players or more). The usual size is about 16 players. They play **cornets, horns, trombones,** and **euphoniums** of different sizes. There is usually a drummer, who also plays percussion.

Nowadays, brass band playing flourishes everywhere. Bands play at parades, take part in competitions and music festivals, and travel to give concerts all over the country. Many schools and colleges have fine bands of their own.

Instruments and Orchestras

This mechanical instrument sounds like a violin and piano playing together. Although there are three violins, each has only one string, played by a bow which moves automatically from one to the other

How instruments work

▲ The humming bird's wings vibrate so fast that they make a whirring or humming sound

▲ Sound waves are something like the ripples made by these boiling mud-pools in Rotorua, New Zealand

What is sound?

If you go outside on a still day, when there is no wind, and nothing is moving, you will hear very little sound at all. Then, if you shout or clap hands sharply, you should hear the sound coming back to you in the stillness. This is called an **echo**, and the ripples of sound you hear are called sound waves.

Those sound waves are caused by movements of the air. Your shouting or clapping makes the air **vibrate** (that is, move or shudder in rapid patterns). The air-vibrations make our ear-drums vibrate, and our brains turn that vibration into the sound we hear.

Why there are different sounds

The sort of sound we hear depends on the way the air vibrates. The way you make the sound causes the air to vibrate in a particular way, and produces sound waves of a particular shape or size. Each wave-shape tells the ear what kind of sound it is hearing. (In the box below, you can see the different wave-shapes made by a whistle, a clap, and a thud.)

The number of **wave vibrations** is important to the sound. When a car is standing still, with the engine running, the engine-noise is quite low, and you can hear each separate throb. When the car begins to move, the throbs get faster and faster, and gradually merge to make what sounds like a single note, much higher than before. Sound waves work in the same way: the *faster* the vibrations, the *higher* the note. If you play the lowest note on a piano, and hold it down, you may be able to hear the throb of the vibrating air. But if you play the highest note, the throbbing is too fast for any human ear, and all you hear is a single sound.

Each particular note of music has its own special number of vibrations. For example, when you hear an orchestra **tuning up** (that is, getting the instruments in tune with each other, so that the notes don't jangle or buzz), they all use the same tuning note, A above middle C. Musicians have agreed that when this A is 'in tune', it has 440 vibrations per second. Any more, or any less, and the note sounds 'out of tune'.

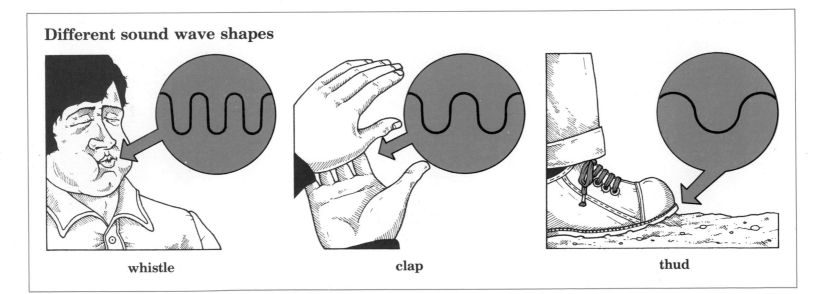

Different sound wave shapes

whistle   clap   thud

Plain sounds and rich sounds

As well as the main note we hear, there is a cloud of quieter, shadowing notes which sound at the same time. These are called **overtones**. Our ears know they are there, but can hardly hear them on their own. They add colour and richness to the basic note. Some instruments (like wood blocks) make very few overtones, and so produce a dull, plain note. Others (like cellos) make many overtones, and produce a rich, full sound.

You can test the effect of overtones by tapping a pen gently against an empty glass or bottle. If you tap freely, there is a rich, ringing sound. But if you put one finger on the glass, and then tap, you cut off some of the overtones. The glass still makes the same basic note; but with the overtones removed its sound is duller.

Kinds of instruments

We can make many different sounds ourselves, just by using mouth and fingers. If you make a narrow opening in your lips, and blow through it, you produce a whistle. If you open your lips to make a small 'o' shape, and then tap your cheeks with your finger, you should get a small, hollow sound like a tiny drum. (By making the 'o' of your lips bigger or smaller, you may be able to make higher or lower notes – because you are changing the shape of the vibrating air.) If you stroke or scratch your cheeks, you get a different kind of sound again.

Blowing, tapping, stroking — each method of 'playing' produces a different kind of sound. Musical instruments work in the same way. Some (like trumpets or flutes) are *blown*; others (like drums or piano-strings) are *tapped*; others (like violin-strings) are *stroked* or *plucked*. You can blow, tap, or stroke as softly or as hard as you like. The more softly you play, the gentler vibrations you make, and the softer the actual sound.

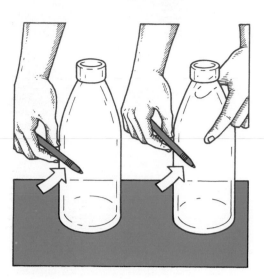

▲ Two different sounds made by tapping a bottle: vibrating and muffled

▲ Sounds you can make yourself

blown

tapped

stroked/plucked

More about
how voices work D2-3
instruments C4, C7, C11, C14-15

C3

Woodwind instruments

Woodwind instruments got their name because they were made of wood, and played with wind (by blowing). Once, there were dozens of different kinds. Some had strange shapes, and even stranger names: for example, **crumhorn, bladder-pipe, phagotum, rackett**. Many have now died out, but others are still used today, especially in concerts of 'early music' (that is, music up to about the 18th century). If you play the **recorder**, you are using one of the oldest types of wind instruments still known. Instruments like our recorders were placed in Egyptian pyramids over 5000 years ago – and some have been found in good condition, and could still be played today.

In most modern orchestras, four kinds of woodwind instruments are used. They are **flutes, oboes, clarinets** and **bassoons**. When musicians talk about 'the woodwind', these are the instruments they mean.

◄ Medieval wind instruments: recorders, crumhorns and a rackett (carved on the bell of an old wooden oboe)

▲ Two trumpets and a shawm (ancient oboe) from the Middle Ages

Keys

A modern woodwind instrument is covered with **keys** and **levers**. This is to help the player reach all the notes. Some of the holes are a long way from the player's fingers (on a bassoon, some are over one metre away). They are awkward to reach and play, especially in fast music. The levers and keys close these awkward holes. (If you try working the keys on a flute or a clarinet, you will see how ingenious the system is.)

▼ How the levers on a flute work. Pressing lever 1 works the key which gives you the note G sharp. Lever 2 helps you play C sharp and C

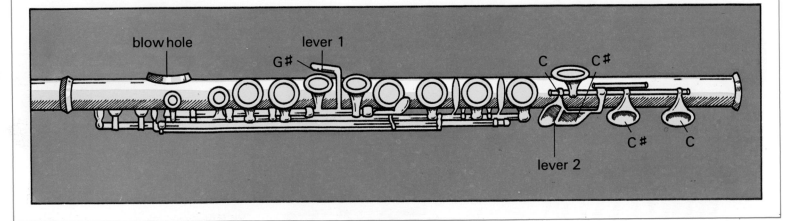

blow hole   lever 1   G♯   C   C♯   C♯   C   lever 2

Flute

A flute player

You hold the flute in a different way from all the other woodwind instruments. Instead of blowing down into it from the top, you hold it sideways, and blow across a hole with a sharpened edge. The way you aim your breath controls the sound.

There are usually at least two flutes in a full-size modern orchestra. Most orchestras use a **piccolo** as well. This is a half-size flute, and plays higher, shriller notes.

A piccolo player

▲ Flute tune, *Dance of the Reed Pipes,* from Tchaikovsky's ballet *The Nutcracker*

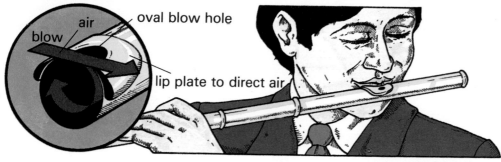

air
oval blow hole
blow
lip plate to direct air

▲ How sound is made in a flute

Oboe

An oboe player

You make the sound in an oboe by blowing down into it. Your breath passes through a mouthpiece made of two strips of flat cane bound together. This is called a **reed**. It gives the oboe a plaintive, rather spiky sound.

There are usually at least two oboes in an orchestra. Sometimes a **cor anglais** (kor ON-glay), or 'English horn', is used as well. This is a larger oboe, playing lower notes.

Adagio (Slowly)

dolce (sweetly)

▲ Oboe tune from the second movement of Brahms' violin concerto

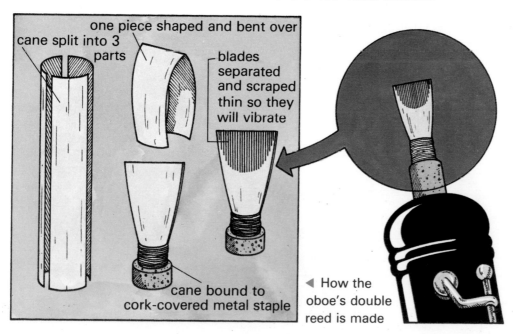

one piece shaped and bent over
cane split into 3 parts
blades separated and scraped thin so they will vibrate
cane bound to cork-covered metal staple

◄ How the oboe's double reed is made

A cor anglais player

C5

Clarinet

The clarinet has a **single reed**, one piece of cane fastened to the mouthpiece by a metal clip. When you blow into the clarinet, your breath passes between this reed and the flat side of the mouthpiece. The sound of the clarinet is silky and rich lower down, smooth in the middle, and piercing higher up.

There are usually at least two clarinets in an orchestra. As well as the normal size, there are **piccolo clarinets** (smaller), and **bass clarinets** (larger). Clarinet players often play the **saxophone** as well. This is rare in orchestras, but common in jazz bands, military bands, and sometimes pop. It makes a noise rather like a clarinet, but thinner and more reedy.

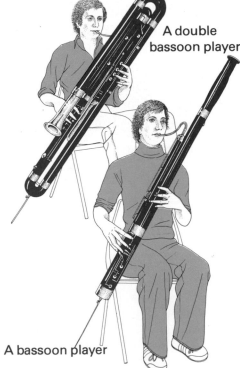

A clarinet player

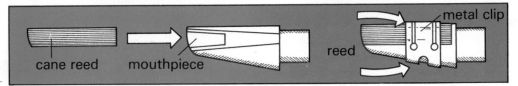

▲ The tune of the slow movement from Mozart's Quintet for clarinet and strings

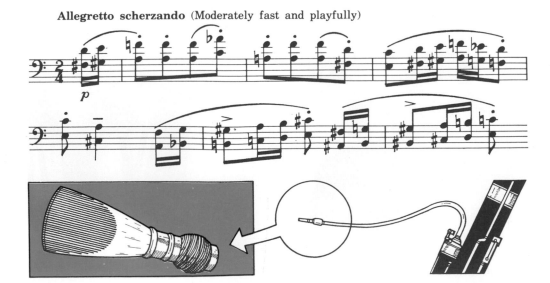

◀ Fixing the clarinet reed into the mouthpiece

Bassoon

Because the bassoon is so large (over three metres), it is divided into two sections, which are bent round and fastened side by side. This brings the blowing end to the middle, near your mouth. When you play, your breath passes first through a **double reed** (like the oboe's but much larger), and then through a short metal pipe called a **crook**, down into the instrument. Low down, the bassoon sounds rich and full; higher up it makes a thinner, more plaintive sound.

There are usually at least two bassoons in an orchestra. In some orchestras, a **double bassoon** is used as well. This is a huge instrument. The tube is over five metres long, and has to be bent into three parts to make it possible for the player to hold it. The double bassoon plays the lowest notes of all the woodwind instruments.

A double bassoon player

A bassoon player

◀ Two bassoons play this tune from the second movement of the *Concerto for Orchestra* by the Hungarian composer Bartók

◀ The bassoon's reed and crook

More about woodwind instruments C4-5

Brass instruments

Brass instruments are often used when magnificent, ceremonial music is needed. They are ideal for fanfares, hunting-calls, and military music. They are made of metal, copper-plated or silver-plated, and often polished until they glow.

In the modern orchestra, four main kinds of brass instruments are used: **trumpets, horns, trombones** and **tubas.**

▲ A 16th-century horn

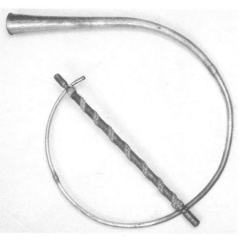

▲ A Roman war-horn called a cornu

▲ A serpent: a low-voiced wind instrument, named after its wriggly shape

Slides and valves

Brass instruments are long tubes of metal (up to five metres long), coiled round to make them easier to hold. The player can change the length of the basic tube, to help himself get more notes. On a trombone, he does this by sliding one piece of tube (actually called the **slide**) in and out of another. On the other brass instruments, he presses down keys called **valves**, which open up extra lengths of tube. He can also make different notes by changing the shape of his lips as he blows. Each different lip-position produces a different note.

▼ How a trumpet's valve works

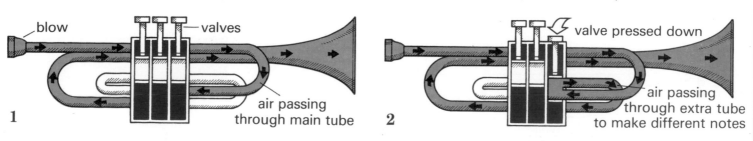

blow — valves

air passing through main tube

1

valve pressed down

air passing through extra tube to make different notes

2

Trumpet

The trumpet is made of a coiled metal tube about 130 cm long. To make the sound, you squeeze your lips across a special **mouthpiece**, and blow. There are usually two, three, or four trumpets in an orchestra. Most trumpet players can play the **cornet** as well.

Trumpets have a clear, bright sound. You can change this to a quieter, rather muffled sound by putting a cardboard or plastic **mute** into the 'bell' of the instrument (the end furthest from the mouth). Ordinary mutes are shaped like huge ice-cream cones; there are other types as well, called 'cup mutes', 'wow-wow mutes', and 'plunger mutes'. Each affects the sound in a different way.

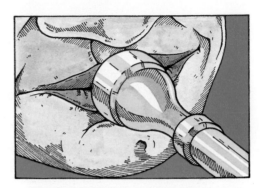

▲ Fitting the lips to a trumpet mouthpiece

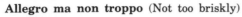

Allegro ma non troppo (Not too briskly)

▲ This trumpet fanfare begins the last movement of the Eighth Symphony by the Czech composer Dvořák

◄ A trumpet player

straight   cup   wow-wow

▲ Trumpet mutes

Horn (sometimes called 'French horn')

The horn is made of a coiled metal tube nearly four metres long. You make the sound in the same way as on a trumpet, though the horn mouthpiece is a different shape. You support the horn's weight by putting one hand in the 'bell' end. This hand can also be used as a mute, to muffle and change the sound. (There are artificial mutes as well, but the hand is just as good, and is just as often used.)

Often, when horn players have no notes to play, you can see them turn their instruments upside-down and empty out small amounts of water. The reason is that when the player's warm breath touches the cold metal inside the horn, it turns to tiny water-drops. If he doesn't empty it out, the water soon clogs the sound.

There are usually four horns in an orchestra.

▲ A horn player

Allegro non troppo (not too briskly)

▲ This horn tune opens Brahms' Second Symphony

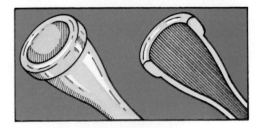

▲ Horn mouthpiece (longer and narrower than a trumpet's)

Trombone and tuba

Although trombones and tuba are actually two quite different kinds of instrument, they are usually grouped together in the orchestra. They play the lowest notes of the brass. There are usually three trombones and one tuba.

You make the sound on a **trombone** by blowing into a mouthpiece, in the same way as on a horn or trumpet. You change the notes by using the slide. With the slide right in, the tube is about three metres long. By stretching out your arm, you move the slide out until more than another metre is added to the length. Like all the other brass instruments, the trombone can be played with a mute, if you want a muffled sound.

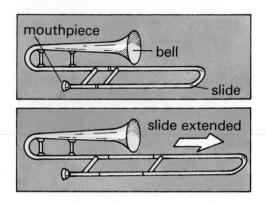

▲ How the slide works on a trombone. The longer the slide, the more notes you can play

◀ A trombone player

▼ This slow tune (a religious chant from the Middle Ages), played by two trombones, begins *The Hymn of Jesus* by the English composer Holst

Senza misura (Freely)

The **tuba** is the largest and heaviest of the brass instruments. It is also one of the youngest (first invented in about 1830). For all its size, it can play surprisingly light, fast notes. Its sound is smooth and rich at the top, and full and round lower down. Its mouthpiece is huge, and covers almost all of the player's lips. Its mute is the size of a large flower pot, big enough for a child to sit on.

▲ A tuba player

Sempre moderato pesante (Steadily and heavily)

▲ This tuba tune, *Bydlo* 'An ox cart', comes from the suite *Pictures at an Exhibition* by the Russian composer Mussorgsky

More about
brass instruments B30-2, C7, C10

bugle

Other brass instruments

Bugle (BYOO-gl)
For giving signals in the army. The tasselled cord goes over the player's shoulder.

Cornet
The chief brass band instrument. Slightly smaller than a trumpet, and slightly easier to play. It can play very fast, agile music, more easily than any other brass instrument.

Baritone
A small-size tuba, used in brass bands and military bands.

Euphonium (yoo-PHONE-ee-um)
This looks like a middle-sized tuba, but it is actually a kind of bugle. It is a favourite brass band instrument, both in this size and in the even bigger **double bass euphonium** size.

Sousaphone (SOOZ-a-phone)
This huge instrument (so big that the player seems almost to be wearing it) was the idea of Sousa, an American band-conductor of the 19th century. It plays the same kind of low notes as a tuba, but is easier to carry as you march. Nowadays most of the coiled part and the bell at the top are made of fibreglass, to keep the weight down even more.

baritone

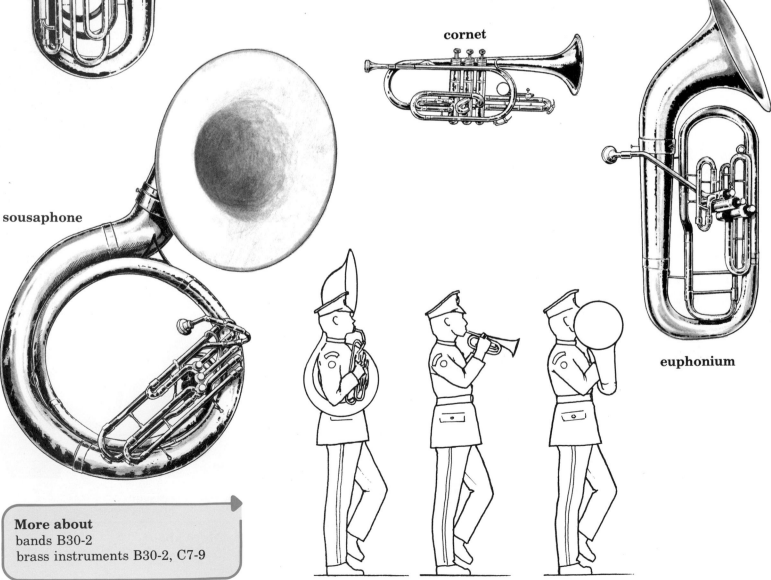

cornet

sousaphone

euphonium

More about
bands B30-2
brass instruments B30-2, C7-9

String instruments

Like woodwind, the family of string instruments is very old. There are string instruments in Stone Age drawings of 10,000 years ago, and instruments not too different from those of today were used 4000 years ago in Egypt and in Ancient Greece.

There are two main kinds of string instruments. In the first kind, you make the sound by moving a **bow** across the strings. The bow is a piece of wood with hairs or threads stretched between the two ends. When you stroke the hairs across the strings, they make the strings vibrate, and this creates the sound.

In other string instruments, you make the sound by *plucking* the strings. The oldest known string instruments were plucked, and plucked instruments are still popular today.

When you play a string instrument, you need only one hand to guide the bow or to pluck the strings. With the fingers of the other hand, you control the *length* of string you need. When the whole string vibrates, it makes its deepest sound. By putting your finger on the string, you stop part of it vibrating, and the shorter vibrating part makes a higher sound. Usually your left hand does the 'fingering' (as this altering of vibration-length is called), while your right hand bows or plucks.

▲ Roman lady plucking a string instrument (from a vase painting)

▼ Two ways of playing a string instrument: with a bow, or by plucking. The third picture shows how the string length is altered by stopping with the fingers

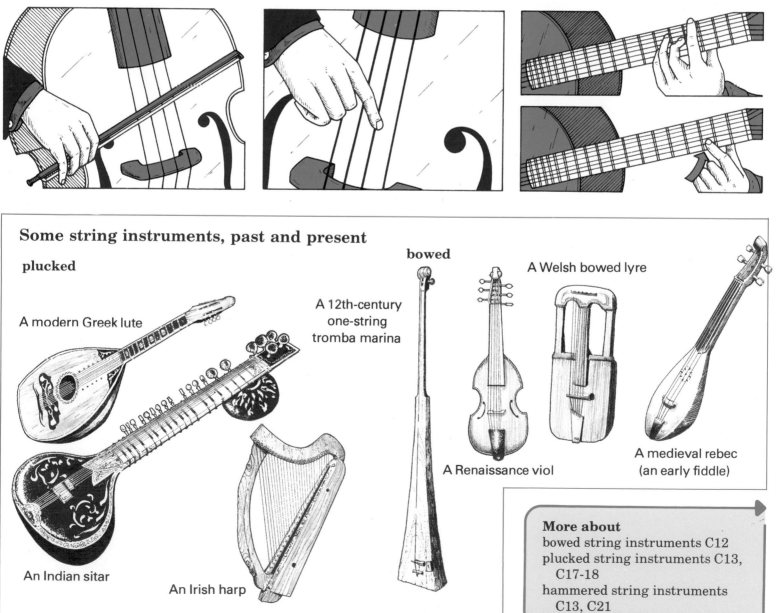

Some string instruments, past and present

plucked

A modern Greek lute

An Indian sitar

An Irish harp

bowed

A 12th-century one-string tromba marina

A Welsh bowed lyre

A Renaissance viol

A medieval rebec (an early fiddle)

More about
bowed string instruments C12
plucked string instruments C13, C17-18
hammered string instruments C13, C21

Bowed instruments

The main string instruments of a modern orchestra are **bowed instruments**. Usually, over half the musicians in an orchestra play strings. They play **violins, violas, cellos** (short for violoncellos) and **double basses**.

▼ A lively piece of violin music: the beginning of Bach's *Partita in E* for solo violin

VIOLIN

VIOLA SOLO

Andante comodo (At a comfortable walking pace)
cantabile espressivo (singing and expressively)

▲ The dreamy, sad opening tune of the Viola Concerto by the English composer William Walton

CELLOS AND DOUBLE BASSES

Allegro moderato (Quite briskly)

con 8va (D.B.)

▲ Cellos and double basses play this tune at the start of Schubert's 'Unfinished' symphony

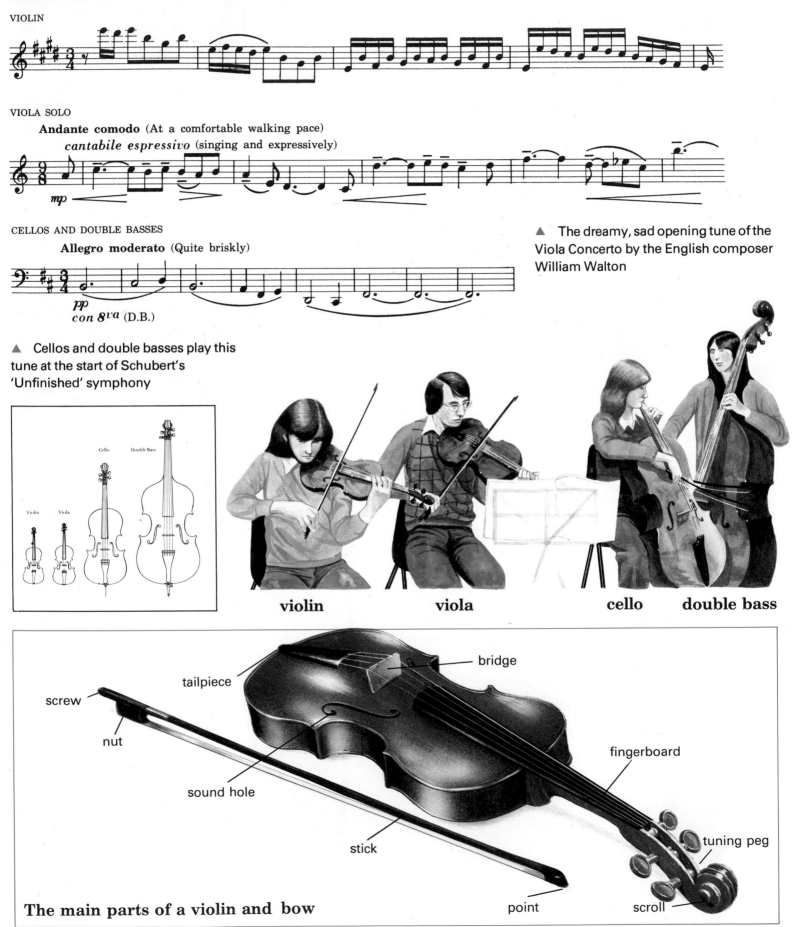

Cello   Double Bass

Violin   Viola

violin   **viola**   **cello**   **double bass**

bridge

tailpiece

screw

nut

fingerboard

sound hole

stick

tuning peg

The main parts of a violin and bow

point   scroll

Plucked instruments

Plucked instruments are rare in orchestras: the sound is too quiet to carry. But they are often used in jazz and pop, and in the home: think of how many people you know who play the guitar. You make the sound either by *plucking* the strings one note at a time, or by *strumming* them (moving your fingers quickly across them, for example to play backing chords in pop or folk music).

Some instruments are always played with the fingers, using the pads at the finger-ends, or the finger-nails. For others, you use a small plucker called a **plectrum**, held between your thumb and first finger. Many instruments, for example the guitar, can use both ways of playing; each way makes a different kind of sound.

◀ Strumming the guitar

GUITAR SOLO

Allegro con spirito (Briskly and with spirit)

◀ The beginning of the *Concierto de Aranjuez* for guitar and orchestra by the Spanish composer Rodrigo (born in 1901). *Rasgueado* tells the guitar player to brush the guitar strings with the back of the finger nails to produce a special Spanish gipsy sound

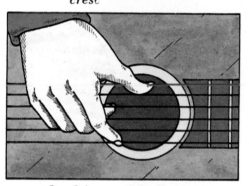

plucking with fingers

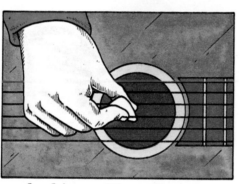

plucking with a plectrum

Strings and hammers

In one family of string instruments, you make the sound not by bowing or plucking the strings, but by hitting them with hammers (which is really plucking turned inside-out). The **dulcimer** is the smallest of these instruments, and the **piano** is the biggest. For the dulcimer, you hold the hammers in your hand; but in the piano, they are worked by keys. You can read more about the piano on page C19 and about the largest member of the dulcimer family, the **cimbalom**, on page C21.

More about
bowed string instruments C12
electric guitars C22
hammered string instruments C21
plucked string instruments C11, C17-18

◀ Cimbalom player. The cimbalom is a Hungarian folk instrument

Percussion instruments

The word percussion (per-KUSH-on) means 'striking'. Out of all the musical instruments in the world, there are probably more sorts of percussion than of any other kind. The basic idea of banging on whatever comes to hand is simple and easy – even young babies can do it well. From that basic idea, the human race has developed a vast range of instruments, and a range of different ways of playing them.

The sound you get depends, first of all, on what the instrument is made of. Wood gives a dry, hollow knocking sound; metal pings or clangs; bone rasps or clicks; pebbles rattle in a jar. Second, the sound depends on how you play the instrument, on whether you *hit, slap, flick, stroke* or *rasp*. And third, it depends on what sort of a 'striker' you use: your hand, for example, makes a different noise from a metal or wooden rod, or a rod tipped with sponge or cloth.

The pictures on this page show a few of the percussion instruments in normal use. Others are being invented all the time. Sometimes they are made from unexpected materials, like car springs, coffee mugs, beer cans, or slates from the roof. You can use anything at all as a percussion instrument, if it makes the sound you want.

▲ Roman carving showing dancer with tambourine

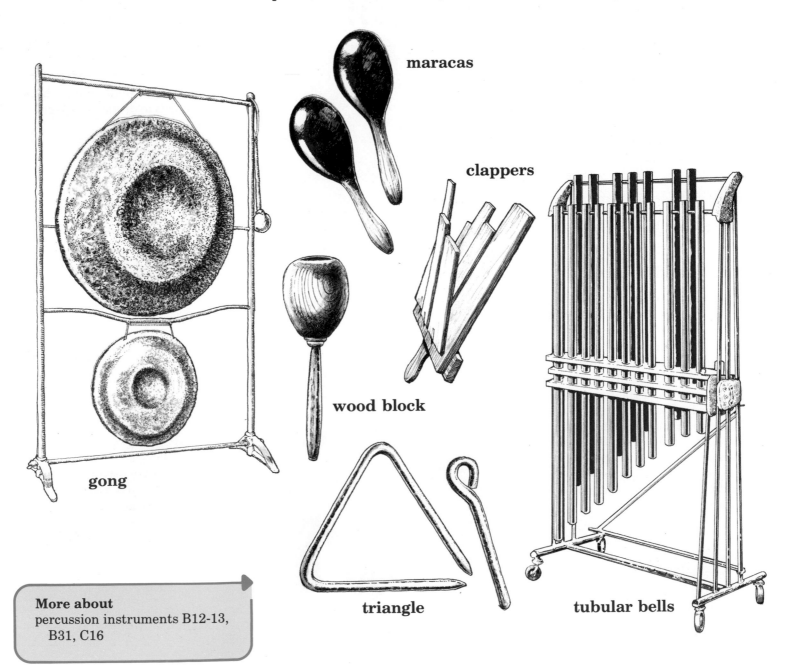

gong

maracas

clappers

wood block

triangle

tubular bells

More about
percussion instruments B12-13, B31, C16

◀ Indian drummer playing a tabla, a pair of drums

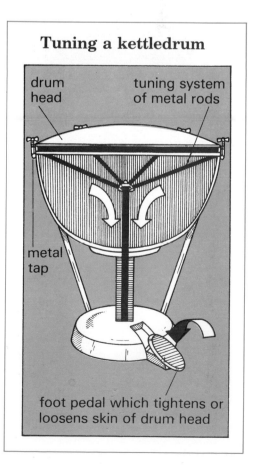

▲ A Yoruba talking drum from Africa, used to send messages in 'drum language'

Drums

The simplest 'drums' of all are ordinary pieces of wood, metal, or stone. When you hit them, they produce a dull thud or clang, with few echoes or overtones. To make a richer sound, you need to make the drum hollow, so that it will *resonate* (that is, create more complicated patterns of vibrating air). You can do this either by hollowing out the basic wood or metal, or by stretching material across the end of a hollow tube. The usual materials are animal skins, cloth (sometimes stiffened with wax or resin), strong paper, and (nowadays) plastic. Whatever the material used, it is called the **skin** of the drum.

The tighter the skin is stretched, the higher the note. Many drums have only one tightness of skin, and only one note. But on others you can change the note as you play, by altering the tightness of the skin. Simply pressing it down will make it change; or you can pull it tighter with cords or metal screws. On orchestral **kettledrums** (so called because their shape is like an old-fashioned cooking-pot, called a 'kettle'), the player often has foot-pedals, which stretch or loosen the skin by means of metal rods. (Older kettledrums have metal taps at the top, which you turn to tighten the skins. Sometimes at concerts you can see a player turning them, then lightly banging the drum and bending over to hear if the new note is the one he wants.)

◀ Playing the kettledrums (timpani)

Tuning a kettledrum

drum head

tuning system of metal rods

metal tap

foot pedal which tightens or loosens skin of drum head

side drum

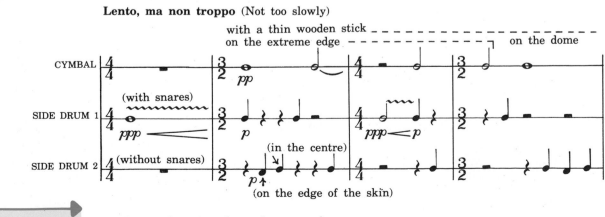

tom tom

bass drum

drum kit

In orchestras, apart from kettledrums, the main drums are **side drum, bass drum,** and different sizes of **tom tom.** These are the drums of a **drum kit,** too (that is, the set of drums used in jazz and pop). The bass drum is worked by a foot-pedal, and the player uses wooden drumsticks, sponge-headed sticks, and sometimes wire brushes, to play the other drums. Military bands and marching bands use mainly side drums and bass drums. (The 'side drum' originally got its name because it was slung at the player's side.) In some cavalry bands there is a kettledrummer. He sits on horseback, with the drums slung on either side of him.

The players

In an orchestra, the chief percussion player plays the kettledrums (also known by the Italian word for drums, **timpani,** TIM-pan-i). All the other percussion instruments are shared out among several other players. They need to be quick-thinking, and quick-moving too. There can be dozens of instruments involved, from tiny **finger-cymbals** to gigantic **gongs,** from **maracas** to **vibraphones.** For a concert audience, part of the fun is watching the percussion players, as they put one instrument down, and creep as quietly as they can to the next, ready to play it when the moment comes.

▲ Kettledrummers (and patient horses) in the cavalry band

Lento, ma non troppo (Not too slowly)

▲ Percussion parts from the second movement
Sonata for two pianos and percussion by the Hungarian composer
Bartók, showing different ways of playing the instruments

More about
military band instruments B30-1

Harp

Harps come in many shapes and sizes, from small hand-harps to the large concert harps used in classical music. They have always been favourite instruments for folk music. In some African religions, the harp was regarded as a magic instrument; in Europe, people believed that harps were instruments played by angels in heaven. Most orchestras have one harp; large orchestras sometimes have two.

▶ Harp player

▲ A painting of a harp player from ancient Egypt

The harpist in an orchestra leans the harp against the right shoulder, and plucks the strings with both hands. There are seven pedals, which change the length of the strings and so alter the notes they play (the shorter the string, the higher the note). As well as plucking the strings, you can sweep both hands very quickly backwards and forwards across them. This makes a rippling sound, hard to produce on any other instrument.

Tempo di Valse (In waltz time)

▲ Harp lesson in 18th-century France

◀ This rush of notes on the harp begins the Flower Waltz from the closing scene of Tchaikovsky's ballet *The Nutcracker*

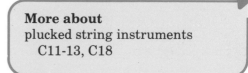
More about
plucked string instruments
C11-13, C18

The harp is a difficult instrument to keep in tune. Often before a concert, the harpist is on the platform half an hour early, tuning and adjusting the strings before any other players arrive.

Keyboard instruments

Keys

All keyboard instruments have **keys**. The keys are levers, and you press them down to make the sound. Each key causes a string to sound its own particular note. The strings and keys are arranged with the notes in order, from lowest (on the player's left) to highest (on his right).

Plucked strings

The main keyboard instruments using plucked strings are **harpsichord, spinet** and **virginals**. The harpsichord is the largest. Very often it has two keyboards, each working a different set of strings. The spinet and virginals are smaller and quieter. (Some virginals are only the size of a large suitcase, and can be played on a table-top.)

▲ A spinet

▲ This virginals belonged to Queen Elizabeth I

▶ Harpsichord: its beautiful decorations make it a valuable piece of furniture as well as a musical instrument

In each of these instruments, pressing down a key moves a small piece of leather, thin metal, or quill (the hard part of a bird's feather) called a **plectrum** to pluck the string.

▶ How the harpsichord works. (1) When you press the key the damper moves away from the string and the plectrum, set in the jack, plucks it. (2) When you let go the key the plectrum falls back and the damper stops the string sounding

More about
piano E22
keyboard instruments C20-2
plucked instruments C11-13,
  C17, C22
harpsichord E16

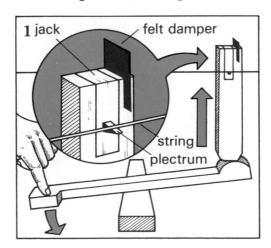

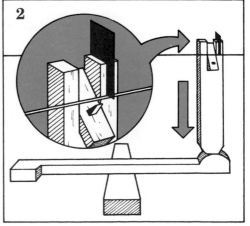

1 jack   felt damper

string
plectrum

2

Clavichord and piano

The **clavichord** (KLAV-i-kord) is the smallest and quietest of all the keyboard instruments. When you press down a key, a small metal bar, like the end of a screwdriver, rises up to touch the string. The noise is as soft as if you pinged the strings gently with your finger-nail. The clavichord is not a public instrument; it is best enjoyed by a very few people, or by the player himself, in a quiet room.

The **piano** is quite different: a powerful instrument whose sound can fill the largest hall. But as its full name shows (*pianoforte*, pyan-o-FOR-tay, Italian for 'soft-loud'), it can play quietly and delicately too.

There are two sorts of piano. **Grand pianos** are normally used in halls and large buildings. But for smaller rooms, an **upright piano** is more usual. It works in the same way as a grand, but has its strings upright instead of laid out flat.

When you press down the piano key, a felt-edged **hammer** hits the string or strings (some of the notes have as many as three strings each). To stop the strings jangling, and one set of sounds jostling another, the strings are touched by felt fingers called **dampers**. When you press down a key, the damper moves away from the string and allows it to sound. When you let the key go, the damper touches the string again, and stops the sound. If you want to play really softly, you press the **left-hand pedal** as you play. On a grand piano, this moves the hammers along a short way, so that they strike only one string instead of three. On an upright, it moves a strip of felt across the strings to quieten them, or moves the hammers much nearer the strings, so that they strike them much less hard. But if you want the sound to last when your fingers have left the keys, you press the **right-hand pedal** as you play. This lifts the dampers from all the strings at once. This pedal is sometimes called the 'sustaining pedal', because it 'sustains' (that is, keeps on) the sound.

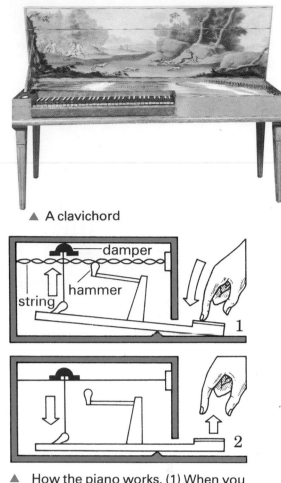

▲ A clavichord

▲ How the piano works. (1) When you press the key the hammer hits the string and the damper moves away. (2) When you let go the key the hammer falls back and the damper stops the string sounding

▼ How the soft pedal works on a grand piano. (a) When the soft pedal is not being used the hammer strikes three strings. (b) With the soft pedal down the hammers all move and strike only one string

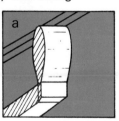

▼ upright piano   ▼ grand piano

▼ The beginning of *Study in C sharp minor* by Chopin, one of the most famous composers of piano music

Presto (Fast) *con fuoco* (with fire)

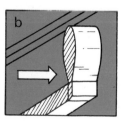

▲ The painted pipes of the organ of an English parish church

Pipe organ

Organs are huge wind instruments, with rows and rows of pipes, each tuned to a different note. A mechanical blower sends wind to the pipes. When you press down a key, the bottom of the pipe opens to let the wind go through, and that makes the sound. Let the key go, and the pipe-bottom closes to stop the sound.

Organs can have many keyboards. Four is common, and six or seven are possible (more would be outside most players' reach). All the keyboards except one are played by the hands, and are called **manuals.** The odd one out is the **pedal keyboard**, played by the feet. On most organs, there are many more sets of pipes than there are keyboards. To play a different set, you press a switch or pull a handle called a **stop**. This connects the set of pipes you want with the keys you play.

▶ The opening of Bach's chorale prelude for organ based on the carol *In dulci jubilo*. Notice that the top and bottom lines both have the tune

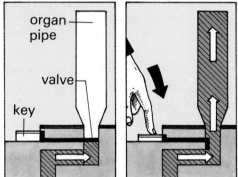

▲ How pressing a key lets air into an organ pipe

▶ A modern church organ

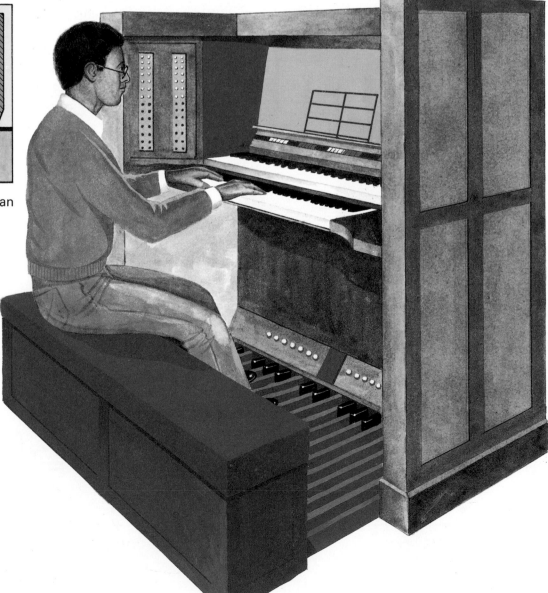

Unusual sounds

Celesta (se-LES-ta)

This looks like a very small piano. Instead of strings the hammers strike thin metal bars. The sound is a gentle, quiet chime. The most famous piece for celesta comes in *The Dance of the Sugar-plum Fairy* from the ballet *The Nutcracker* by Tchaikovsky.

celesta

Cimbalom (SIM-ba-lom)

This is a Hungarian folk instrument, and belongs to the **dulcimer** family. It looks like the strings from an opened-up piano, laid on a table. The player holds hammers in his hands, and uses them to strike the strings. The sound is quiet and rather jangling – the sort of sound you get by plucking the strings inside an ordinary piano. The most famous piece using a cimbalom is the *Háry János Suite* by Kodály.

cimbalom

Xylophone (ZY-lo-phone)

The xylophone is a set of wooden blocks, each sounding a different note. They are laid out in the same way as piano keys. You play them by hitting them with wooden hammers. The sound is dry, brittle, and rattling. In Saint-Saëns's *Danse Macabre* the rattling xylophone is used to suggest skeletons dancing in a graveyard.

Vibraphone (VY-bra-phone)

You play the vibraphone very like a xylophone. It consists of metal bars, laid out like piano keys, and struck with soft hammers. Underneath each bar is an electrically-operated **resonator**: this holds the sound on and makes it vibrate or wobble. As well as in orchestras, vibraphones are often used in jazz.

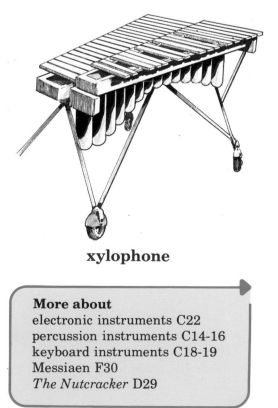

xylophone

Ondes martenot (on-de-MAR-ten-oh)

An electronic musical instrument. It makes a wobbling, sliding sound, rather like a musical saw. Many French composers have used it in orchestral works. The most famous is *Turangalîla* by Messiaen.

vibraphone

ondes martenot

More about
electronic instruments C22
percussion instruments C14-16
keyboard instruments C18-19
Messiaen F30
The Nutcracker D29

Electronic instruments

Until this century, all instruments needed men's help to make the sound waves. Men blew, tapped or stroked, and vibrating air made the sound. But nowadays, there are **electronic instruments** which can make sound waves without man's help. A favourite is the **electric organ**. This has no pipes, no blower, no wind. When you press down a key, an electric circuit is completed, and this generates (that is, creates) the sound.

All electronic instruments pass their sound through loudspeakers. Pop groups often use electronic instruments (like the **synthesizer**), and also ordinary instruments (guitars, flutes, violins) amplified by electricity and making their sound through loudspeakers. The sound they make is changed by using three electronic devices. **Vibrators** repeat it very fast, and so make it last as long as you like; **modulators** change the shape of the sound wave, and so vary the basic sound; **fuzz-boxes** change the 'overtones' (see page C2), and so make the sound blur or buzz.

Synthesizer

A synthesizer (SINTH-e-size-er) is an electronic instrument with a built-in computer. When you press down a key, a basic sound is generated, just as in an electric organ. But then, once the sound is made, by pressing switches and turning knobs, you can instruct the computer to change the basic sound wave into any new shape you like – and each new shape is a different sound. Synthesizers can imitate the sound waves of any other instruments, as well as making a whole range of sound-patterns all their own.

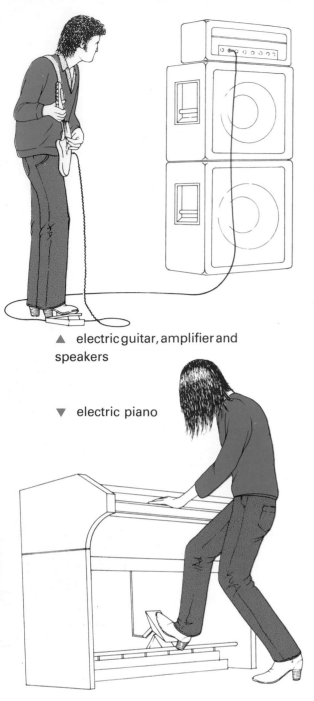

▲ electric guitar, amplifier and speakers

▼ electric piano

▼ synthesizer

▼ Pop guitarist from Steeleye Span with full electronic backing

More about
electronic music G10
pop B26

Unusual instruments

Aeolian harp (ay-OH-lee-an harp)

An excellent instrument for lazy players. You hang it up in a tree or by a window. Any passing breeze vibrates the strings and makes the instrument sound. Aeolian harps were common in temples and gardens in the Far East, especially in India, Java, Tibet, and China. (You can make one yourself, with thin rubber bands or wires stretched over a slot cut in a cereal packet or small cardboard box.)

Walking-stick flute

Use it for walking. Then, when you feel like a tune, put it to your lips and play. There are walking-stick guitars and violins as well.

Musical glasses

Glasses filled with different amounts of water. You play them by rubbing a wet finger gently around the rims. A popular instrument in Vienna 250 years ago. Mozart wrote two pieces for it. (You can make a simpler one yourself, using old bottles or jam jars. Eight will make a scale. Play them by tapping gently with a fork.)

Musical saw

An ordinary large saw, bent round and played with a violin or cello bow. If the angle is right, you get a high, eerie wailing noise. Skilful performers can play tunes. The saw is sometimes used for ghostly singing in horror films. (If you try this, be careful: it won't work unless you have the right kind of bow, and the saw tends to spring about, and could slap back into your face.)

Musical suitcase

For this, you need a suitcase, a broom handle, a piece of string or wire, and a staple. You open the suitcase, and fasten one end of the string into a corner. Then you stand the broom handle in the opposite corner, staple the free end of the string to the top, and make sure it's tight. (The tighter you get the string, the better the notes will be.) You now have a simple double bass, for plucking. This instrument was actually used by poor jazz players about 50 years ago. In the 1950s, people made basses out of tea chests and cardboard boxes, in just the same way. (If you try one of your own, it's best to use a box or tea chest, rather than risk damaging the family luggage.)

More about unusual sounds C21

C23

The orchestra

An **orchestra** (OR-kes-tra) is a large group of musicians, playing many different instruments. The instruments belong to four main 'families': **woodwind, brass, percussion,** and **strings**.

Orchestras vary in size, from small (under 30 players) to very large (over 100 players). The picture opposite shows a standard-size orchestra of about 80 players. In the diagram you can see where each group of players sits.

In most buildings, the orchestra sits with the louder instruments at the back, and the quieter instruments at the front. That means that the listener hears a 'balanced' sound, without some instruments swamping the others. (In recording studios, or places like cathedrals, where not all the audience sit facing the front of the orchestra, the arrangement of the orchestra seats can be different from this diagram. But in most concert-halls this kind of seating-plan is used.)

How many of each instrument are used? It depends on loudness and quietness of sound. There are far more of each quiet instrument (for example, strings) than of louder ones (for example, brass). The size of an instrument does not always affect the loudness or clearness of its sound. The double bass, for example, is very quiet, and its sound is easily drowned. A triangle, on the other hand, makes such a distinctive sound that you can hear it easily even when every other instrument in the orchestra is playing as well.

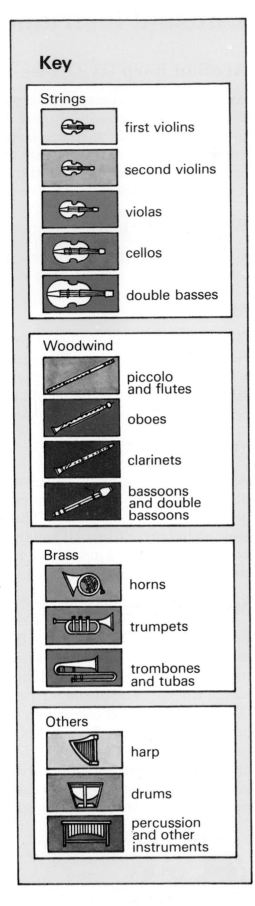

How many of each instrument?

These are the numbers in the basic, normal orchestra. For special works, there can be many more. The composer Mahler, for example, used so many players and singers in his Eighth Symphony that it was nicknamed 'Symphony of a Thousand'.

Woodwind (10 players)
1 piccolo
2 flutes
2 oboes
2 clarinets
2 bassoons
1 double bassoon

Brass (11 players)
4 horns
3 trumpets
3 trombones
1 tuba

Strings (54 players)
24 violins, divided into two groups of 12 ('first violins' and 'second violins')
12 violas
10 cellos
8 double basses

Others (4 players)
1 harp
3 or 4 kettledrums (1 player)
many percussion instruments (2 players)

Total: 79 players

More about
instruments of the orchestra
   C5-17, C21
orchestras C26-30, C32
writing down orchestral music
   G8-9

▼ A modern symphony orchestra (in the Royal Festival Hall, London). You can
see from the diagram where players of each group of instruments sit

The orchestra at work

Concerts

At a concert, the orchestra plays in front of an audience. Concerts are given in schools, churches, theatres, and in town and village halls. Many large cities have concert-halls, built especially for musical performances.

Sometimes, in a concert, other musicians join the orchestra. It could be one or more **soloists**, playing a concerto; or it could be a **choir**, joining the orchestra to perform a choral work. The orchestra also plays on its own, in overtures, symphonies, and suites.

The theatre

Most operas and ballets need a full-size orchestra. Some companies have full-time orchestras of their own; others use visiting orchestras. Stage musicals, and sometimes plays, use orchestras as well. In the theatre, the orchestra plays in a special place called the 'pit', under the front of the stage. Some pit orchestras are small, just a handful of players; others (like those for the operas of Wagner or Richard Strauss) can have more than 100 musicians.

▲ The American composer Aaron Copland conducting a school choir. You can read more about him on page F28 of *Composers and their Music*

▼ A few members of the string section of a school orchestra

Films, television, and radio

Films, television, and radio programmes often use background music or **incidental music**. It helps to set the mood of a scene, and to give it the right atmosphere. (Think, for example, how romantic music helps a love-scene, or how eerie music is used for ghosts, or how fast-moving music can add excitement to a chase.) Many television and radio programmes also have **signature-tunes**, special music to begin or end the show. Sometimes all this music is taken from records; but very often it is written especially for the programme, and recorded on film or tape by a studio orchestra.

The recording studio

If you look through the records in your house, you may be surprised at how many of them use an orchestra. Orchestras make records of their own. But they often appear with musicians of other kinds. (The Beatles; Rod Stewart; Elton John – listen to the 'backing' when they sing or play. Sometimes a few instruments are playing, sometimes a large orchestra.)

Musicians who play 'backing' music are hired for one recording session at a time, and so are called 'session players'. They also provide the music for **jingles** and **commercials**. Session playing is varied and interesting work, and gives the player the chance to play many different kinds of music.

▲ A soloist and orchestra recording a piano concerto. The pianist is the Brazilian Cristina Ortiz. You can find out more about her on page C31.

More about
choirs D5-7
concerts E20, E26, G14
films B21, B27, D22-5
recording B28-9
soloists C31, D4
music in the theatre B15,
    B18-19, D8-9, D13-14, D16, D22,
    D30-31, E17

Leader and conductor

Leader

The chief player in an orchestra is called the **leader** (in America, **concert-master**). He plays the violin. When the orchestra *rehearses* (re-HER-ses, that is, practises), his job is to see that everything runs smoothly. He helps the conductor and the players work together to get the sound exactly right. Often there are mistakes to correct in the printed *parts* (the music for each player), and there are musical matters that need a leader's skilled advice. (When you watch an orchestra play, for example, you may notice that the groups of string players move their bows up or down at the same time. A down-stroke produces a slightly stronger sound than an up-stroke. In rehearsal, one of the leader's jobs is to decide, with the conductor, which kind of strokes to use.) Sometimes the leader trains sections of the orchestra in advance, ready for the conductor to take over later.

At the concert, the leader comes on stage when the rest of the orchestra is sitting down, and just before the conductor. He gets a round of applause of his own. He has two jobs in the concert: to play his own part, and to lead the players in carrying out the conductor's signals about playing the music.

▲ The leader (with violin) with the conductor — the Italian Claudio Abbado — discussing some detailed points in the music the orchestra is going to perform

▼ Claudio Abbado conducting the orchestra in rehearsal

Conductor

To the audience, conducting can appear very easy. All you seem to do is stand in front of the orchestra and wave your hands and arms. But to the orchestra these movements are precise signals, which keep it together and remind it of how the conductor wants the music played. As well as arm movements, many conductors use facial expressions (lifted eyebrows, smiles, frowns, and so on) to guide the players. The kind of signals a conductor gives depends on his personality. Some make lively, excited movements; others are still and calm. The kind of movement does not matter, so long as it gets the results the conductor wants.

The conductor's job is to *interpret* the music: that is, to see that it is played exactly as the composer seems to him to want. When different conductors conduct the same piece of music, there can be hundreds of small differences in interpretation: slightly different speeds; tiny slowings-down or speedings-up (musicians call this 'letting the music breathe'); alterations of balance (that is, making some parts of the sound louder or softer than others), and of colour (bringing out the sound of particular instruments). Great conductors often become famous for the way they interpret a particular composer's music.

▲ The Israeli conductor Daniel Barenboim. He is also a pianist, famous for his interpretations of Beethoven and Mozart

◀ The German conductor Eugen Jochum. What do you think he is saying to the orchestra?

How a conductor beats time

Most conductors use a stick called a **baton**. They move it in regular patterns in the air. The patterns are different, according to whether the music has two, three, four, or more beats to the bar. The first beat of each bar is the 'down-beat', because it always goes down; the last beat is the 'up-beat', and always goes up. With his other arm, the conductor makes movements to bring out expression in the playing: loudness, softness, fierceness, or tenderness. He uses his face (especially his eyes) to keep the players' attention and to encourage them to play their best.

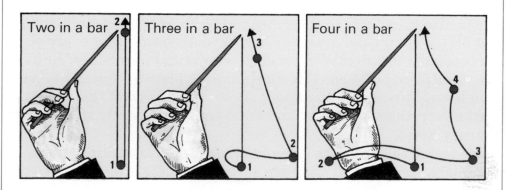

More about
conductors D13
playing and interpreting music G2, G7
rehearsing opera and ballet D10, D13, D31

Behind the scenes

Getting things ready for a concert is a colossal job. There are often more than 100 musicians involved. Each owns an expensive, fragile instrument, which must be transported with the greatest care. Each needs a chair, a music stand, and the right music to play from. If the orchestra has travelled far for the performance, each player will need a meal, and perhaps a hotel room for the night.

The **orchestral manager** makes many of these arrangements. His job is to keep the practical side of things running well, so that the musicians have nothing to worry about except playing the music. He books the hotels, arranges for meals, hires coaches for the players and vans for the instruments, and checks that all the tickets are right before the journey starts. In its own country, an orchestra usually travels by luxury coach; on tours abroad, it goes by plane – and one large orchestra, with all its instruments, can take up most of a large-size jet.

▲ The London Symphony Orchestra on tour. Wheeling in the timpani . . .

▲ . . . loading the players' formal evening clothes on to the orchestra's van

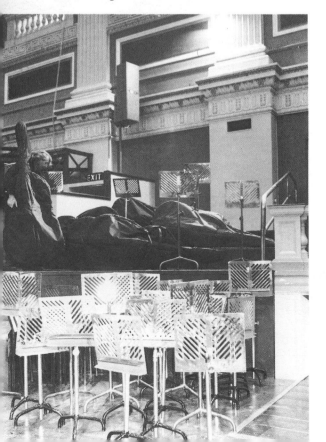

◀ . . . double basses (still in their covers) and music stands waiting to be sorted in the concert-hall

▲ The orchestral librarian putting the parts out on the music stands

The **orchestral librarian** looks after the chairs, music stands and music. He goes early to the rehearsal room or concert-hall, and sets out all the chairs and music stands. He makes sure that every player has enough room to play in comfort. (Harps and trombones, for example, need plenty of space.) He sorts out each player's music (his 'part'), and leaves it ready on the music stand. At the end of the concert, he packs everything up again, and makes sure it is safely stored for the journey home.

No one in the audience sees the manager or librarian at work. But their jobs are essential: they are as important for a successful concert as any player.

Soloists

When you play an instrument really well, you are like a gymnast or an athlete. You have to train your muscles, and to practise and exercise every day to keep up your *technique* (that is, the way you play your instrument). For players of keyboard and string instruments, the finger muscles and arm muscles are most important. Many master-pianists or violinists begin to practise very young (often before they are nine); that way, their muscles are adapting to the instrument all through their growing-time. For wind instruments, the muscles of face and lips are just as important. Your lip muscles have to be quite well grown and firm before you can play a wind instrument really well. For most people, this comes between the ages of about 10 and 12.

Concert soloists travel a good deal. They will certainly tour in their own country, and (if they become well known) they may travel round the world. They stay in each place for only a few days – time to meet the conductor and the orchestra, to try the hall for sound, to rehearse, and to give the performance. Then they set off again, to give another concert somewhere else. As well as touring, many soloists give radio and television performances, make records, and teach, passing on their knowledge and skill to others.

Concert performers give two kinds of concert. First, those with orchestra. In these, they usually play **concertos**. Second, there are concerts called **recitals** (re-SIGHT-als). These are given by the soloists alone, or with one accompanist. In a recital, the soloist often plays **sonatas**.

▲ The life of a concert pianist on tour is tiring, as he or she is constantly on the move. Here Cristina Ortiz waits for a plane at an Italian airport

▲ . . . puts the final touches to her eye make-up while studying the score of the concerto she is about to perform

◀ . . . practises on her own in the hall. Concert pianists have to practise long hours to keep up their technique and learn new works

More about
music for soloists G14
solo singers B20-4, D4

Chamber music

Many concert soloists and orchestral musicians also play **chamber music**. Chamber music uses groups of two to nine players. At first it was music meant for a 'chamber', or room: that is, music for a small group of friends to play to please themselves, or music to entertain a rich man and his guests. Nowadays, many professional groups specialize in playing chamber music, and we hear it in concert-halls. Broadcasts and records of chamber music are particularly good for home listening.

Chamber music works use one player for each part instead of several, as in an orchestra. 18th and 19th-century works often have four movements, and last for about 20–30 minutes. Usually the two outside movements are fast, one of the inside movements is slow, and the other is in dance-style (often a minuet or scherzo).

▲ Four string players and a pianist rehearse a piano quintet, one of the most important kinds of chamber music

Chamber orchestras

When composers write for groups of about 10–30 players, they often say their music is for **chamber orchestra**. The most usual kind of chamber orchestra is a mixture of string and wind instruments, like a small symphony orchestra. Usually it contains woodwind (one or two flutes, oboes, clarinets, and bassoons), brass (often just two horns), timpani (drums), and strings.

A **wind band** or **wind orchestra** is a kind of chamber orchestra that is becoming very popular in schools. It contains woodwind instruments (flutes, oboes, clarinets, bassoons), and sometimes brass (horns, trumpets, trombones).

Kinds of chamber music

Pieces of chamber music usually have names which show the number of players needed. The most common are:

Trio (TREE-oh)
Three players. For example, violin, cello, and piano make up what is called a 'piano trio'.

Quartet (KWOR-TET)
Four players. For example, two violins, viola, and cello make up a 'string quartet'. The string quartets of Haydn, Mozart, Beethoven and Bartók are thought of as some of their best music.

Quintet KWIN-TET)
Five players. The most usual are string quintet (quartet plus one viola or one cello), and wind quintet (flute, oboe, clarinet, bassoon, and horn).

Sextet
Six players, usually all wind or all strings.

Septet
Seven players, usually a mixed group of wind and strings.

Octet
Eight players, usually a mixed group of wind and strings.

Nonet
Nine players, usually a mixed group of wind and strings.

Music for two players is sometimes called a **duo** or **duet**. But most composers call their pieces for two instruments **sonatas** instead.

More about
music for orchestras G12, G14
the symphony orchestra C24-5

Singing and Dancing

Folk singers playing for a dance in the Canary Islands

Our voices and how we use them

What is your voice made of?

In your throat, just under your chin, is a piece of hard, gristly material called the Adam's apple. (It moves up and down when you swallow.) If you put one finger gently on your Adam's apple, at the top, and hold it there while you say a long 'Aaah', you should feel vibrations. These vibrations are the stream of air (called the 'air-column') wobbling as it passes out of your lungs and up towards your mouth. As the air-column vibrates, we can use it to make sounds – and we call these sounds the **voice**.

Vocal cords

The sort of noise we make depends on the shape of the vibrating air-column. We can change the shape, and so change the sound. To change the shape, we use our vocal cords. We have two vocal cords, one on each side of the air-pipe (or 'larynx') that leads from mouth to lungs. The vocal cords are near the top of the air-pipe, just behind the Adam's apple. When we speak or sing we breathe out, and at the same time move our vocal cords to change the size and shape of the opening in the air-pipe. A wide opening lets a wide air-column through, and makes a low note. A narrow opening makes a higher note.

The vocal cords are quite small. In children, they are about 8 mm long. In a grown man they are about 15 mm, and in a woman about 11 mm. That explains why men usually have deeper voices than women or children (because longer vocal cords allow a larger air-column through). Women and children can often make the same high or low sounds; but a woman's voice is usually richer and less piping, because she has slightly longer vocal cords.

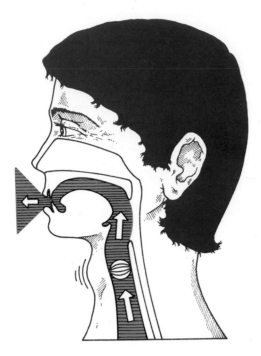

▲ Making the air-column vibrate

▼ Vibrating air column, vocal cords and larynx. You can see three different sizes: man, woman and child

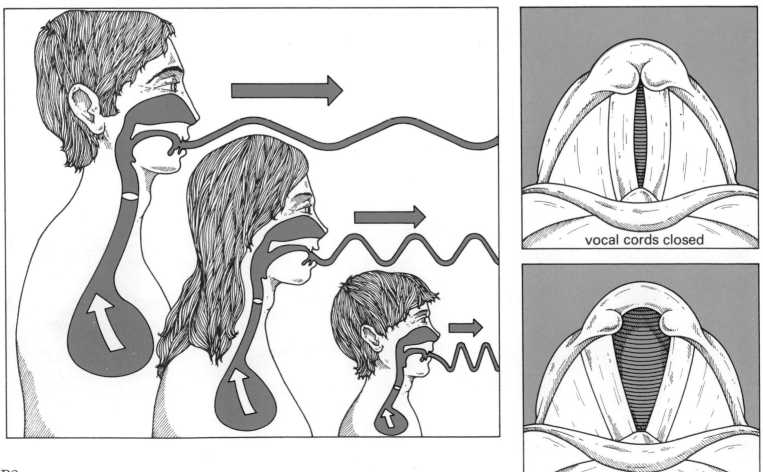

vocal cords closed

vocal cords open

D2

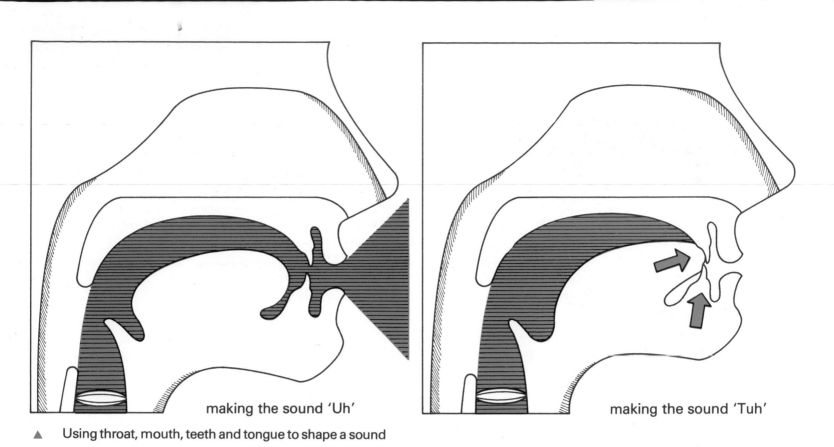

making the sound 'Uh'   making the sound 'Tuh'

▲ Using throat, mouth, teeth and tongue to shape a sound

Throat, mouth, teeth, and tongue

Once the basic sound is made by the vibrating air, it passes up into the throat, mouth, and sinuses (small channels and bony pits in the forehead, and behind the nose). We use our **throat, mouth, teeth,** and **tongue** to shape the sound. (You can feel how this works. Say 'Uh', then 'Tuh'. When you say 'Tuh', it is your teeth and tongue that add a new shape to the basic 'Uh'.) We use our **sinuses** to make the sound rich and echoing. (To hear a sound with some of its echoes removed, hold your nose and say 'Aah'.)

We can make dozens of different kinds of sound, from grunts and squeals to the most delicate singing notes. Good singers learn exact control of their breath (the basic vibrating air-column), and of their vocal cords and the muscles of throat and mouth (which change its shape and produce the final sound). They must be careful of anything which might affect the sinuses (like hay fever, or a cold), as this completely changes the sound they make.

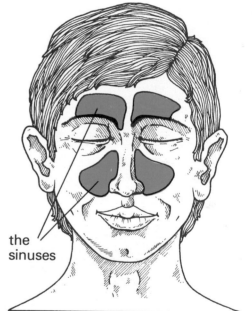

the sinuses

More about
singers B20, B24–6, D4–7
how instruments work C2–3
voices and their music D4, D7, G13

D3

All kinds of singers

Everyone in the human race can sing. But no two voices are ever the same. Just as we like some people and not others, so we have clear ideas about the kind of singing we like or loathe. The same voice can delight some people, and grate on others' nerves. (This is one reason why singers have such eager fans – and why people who dislike a particular singer's voice can never understand what it is his fans adore.)

Professional singers usually wait to start training until they are grown-up. Like players of instruments, they have to practise and exercise every day, to keep their voices in trim. Like players, too, they make their living from concerts, recitals, records, and film and television appearances.

Pop singers and folk singers generally play their own accompaniments, or sing with a backing group. But when a classical singer gives a solo concert or recital, he uses an **accompanist**. The accompanist plays piano (usually), organ, or harpsichord. Many singers work often with the same accompanist, and over the years they grow into a team. The German singer Dietrich Fischer-Dieskau, for example, and the pianist Gerald Moore were a famous partnership in performing Schubert songs.

▲ The opera singer Kiri Te Kanawa from New Zealand

▲ The pop singer David Bowie

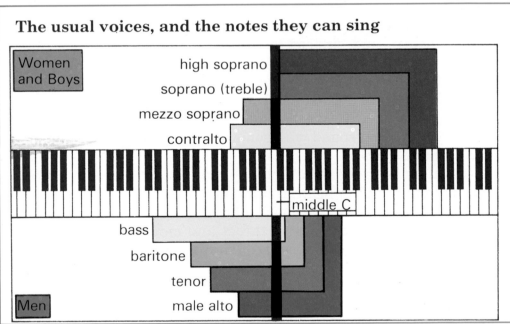

The usual voices, and the notes they can sing

Women and Boys

high soprano
soprano (treble)
mezzo soprano
contralto

middle C

bass
baritone
tenor
Men
male alto

▲ Yodelling in the Swiss mountains

More about
solo instrumental players C31
singers B20, B24–6, D5–7
accompaniment A12

Falsetto and yodelling

Once you are grown-up and your vocal cords have reached their full size, you can use them to produce a kind of trick voice called **falsetto** (fol-SET-oh, an Italian word which here means 'artificial'). To make a falsetto voice, you tighten the vocal cords to produce a very narrow opening. This produces a high-pitched, piping voice. Women can do it as well as men, but it is more clearly heard in men, because it is so much higher than their normal voice. Falsetto is easy to do, but hard to keep up for long. Some men, however, train themselves to sing falsetto regularly. They produce an alto voice (called a **male alto**). You often find male altos in church and cathedral choirs.

In the folk music of some countries (for example Switzerland), people use a singing style called **yodelling**. In this, most of the singing is in a normal, low voice. But every so often the singer 'yodels', that is, breaks into falsetto for a short run of notes. (The name 'yodel' comes from the nonsense-words these singers use, words like 'Yodel-ay-ee-hee'.)

Singing with other people

When you join together with other people to sing, you make a small singing group or a larger **choir** (KWYRE). In a group, there is usually one voice to each line of music: it is like chamber music for voices instead of instruments. In a choir, several voices usually sing each line of music together: it is an orchestra of voices.

The idea of choirs goes back at least 2500 years. In Ancient Greece, choirs of men and boys took part in processions and festivals in honour of the gods, and there were competitions for singing and for choral speaking. The Egyptians and the Romans used choirs in their religious services, and to sing songs at feasts and banquets. In the Middle Ages, choirs were used in churches, many palaces and some large houses. Nowadays most churches and schools have choirs. Choral singing is a popular musical hobby, and choirs of every kind give concerts, and perform on television, radio, and records.

A choir can be of any size, from small (about 12 voices) to very large (200 voices or more). Music for voices is called **vocal music**, and music for choirs is usually called **choral music**. On the next page you will find the opening bars of one of the most famous pieces of choral music ever written, Handel's *Hallelujah Chorus*.

▲ Singing in choirs is a popular hobby (and as this cartoon shows, often a noisy one)

▶ A church choir today. Men and boys of the choir of Christ Church cathedral, Oxford, wearing red cassocks and white surplices

▼ A church choir from the Middle Ages singing mass

▲ Choirboys from Ancient Rome

More about
choirs D6–7
choral music A16, G13
music at school E28–29

Church music and church choirs

Most religions, throughout the world, make use of music. Sometimes they use **chant**. In this, the priest sings the words of prayers to a fixed pattern of just a few repeated notes. Chanting helps the priest's words to be clearly heard, and also makes his voice sound more solemn and dignified. At other times, all the worshippers join in the chants. In Christian churches, from the Middle Ages to the present day, the choir has always taken an important part. It leads the singing of the worshippers (for example in **hymns**), and it may also sing parts of the service by itself, music set to sacred words. Some of the greatest music of the West has been written for use in church.

At first, women were not allowed to sing in church choirs. The singers were all male: **choirmen** and **choirboys**. Cathedrals and large churches often had **choir schools**. In these, talented boy singers were given an education, in return for singing in the choir. Many famous musicians (for example the composers Bach, Haydn, Schubert, and Verdi) began their careers as choirboys, and moved on to other kinds of music when their voices broke. Nowadays, some cathedrals still have choir schools, and choirs consisting of men and boys alone. But in most ordinary churches, women and girls are welcome in the choir.

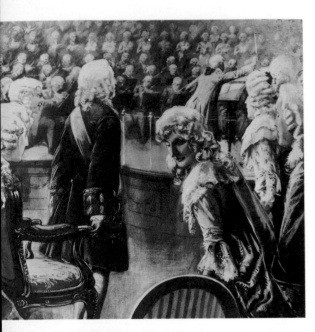

▲ At the first performance of *Messiah*, King George II was so excited by the opening of the Hallelujah Chorus that he jumped to his feet—and all the audience had to do the same. Even now, audiences often stand to hear it

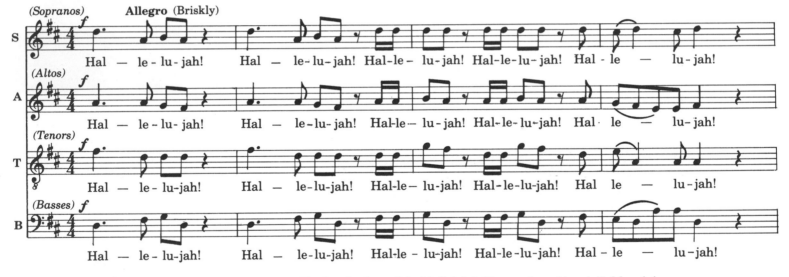

▼ This painting shows the choir of a village church 150 years ago

▲ The beginning of the Hallelujah Chorus from Handel's *Messiah*, showing the parts for all four kinds of voice

▲ A minister leading the congregation in a church service in an American mid-western town

◄ A school choir. These children have treble voices

More about
religious music B2–3, B16
Christian church music A16, E8, E12, E17, G13
voices D4

Some kinds of Christian church music

Hymn (HIM)
A short song with religious words, usually in several verses. The choir and congregation sing the words; the accompaniment is played on the church organ, or (in school assemblies) on piano or guitars. Some well known hymns often sung in schools are *Morning has Broken, O God our Help in Ages Past, He who would valiant be,* and *All Things bright and beautiful.*

Psalm (SAHM)
There are 150 Psalms in the Book of Psalms in the Bible. They are poems and prayers to God. In some churches, the choir and congregation chant psalms as part of the services. The accompaniment is played on the organ. One of the best-known Psalms is Psalm 23, *The Lord is my Shepherd.*

Anthem
A piece of music with religious words, performed in the service by the choir alone, sometimes with organ, sometimes unaccompanied. You may have heard Handel's Coronation anthem *Zadok the Priest,* or Mozart's anthem *Ave Verum.* (Each country in the world has a National Anthem. But this is more like a national hymn that the sort of anthem a church choir sings.)

Cantatas, Passions, Masses
See page G13, *Writing Music*

Voices in the choir

Boys' choir
Trebles (high voices); altos (low voices)

Women's or girls' choir
Sopranos (high voices); altos (medium voices); contraltos (low voices)

Male-voice choir
Tenors (high voices); baritones (medium voices); basses (low voices)

Mixed choir
Sopranos; altos; tenors; basses

Musicians often call these voices by their first letters only. If you talk of an SATB Choir, for example, you mean a mixed choir: Sopranos, Altos, Tenors, Basses.

Opera

What is an opera?

When you watch an opera, it is rather like seeing a play. People act out a story, and play all the parts. But there is an important difference between operas and plays: the music. In an opera, everyone sings instead of speaking, and an orchestra plays throughout the performance. Solo singers act the leading parts, and there is often a **chorus**, a group of people who play villagers, soldiers, courtiers, or whatever other crowds the story needs.

Music is good at suggesting feelings inside us like sorrow, happiness, anger, or despair. In an opera, we find out about the characters of the story in two different ways. We can hear what they say (or rather sing), and see what they do, because it happens in front of us; and at the same time the music tells us something else, the feelings inside their hearts or heads.

Opera can be one of the grandest, most spectacular of all musical entertainments. Many operas use magnificent scenery and costumes, like the one illustrated below. Above all, operas need singers who can act, whose voices have feeling as well as a beautiful sound. (Imagine, for example, you were singing the part of a cruel villain, or a heart-broken lover. You would need to concentrate on the *acting* and at the same time *sing* the music as beautifully as possible.)

▲ Opera, Far Eastern style. These warriors and their prince are characters in an ancient Chinese opera

▼ Opera, Western style. These warriors, dancers and prince are characters in Verdi's opera *Aida,* set in Ancient Egypt

You can sometimes hear operas on the radio, and watch them on television. But the best place to enjoy them is the one they were written for: in the theatre or **opera-house**. Often, an opera-house is specially built for sound, and has an enormous stage, big enough for the huge scenery and large numbers of singers many operas need. As you can see from the picture below, the auditorium (that is, the place where the audience sits) could be beautifully decorated too.

▲ The shell-shaped domes of the Opera House in Sydney, Australia

▼ The Royal Opera House, Covent Garden, London (for a view inside, see the next page)

◄ The auditorium and stage for a grand opera in the 18th century

More about
music for the stage B15, B18–19, C26, D10–17, E17, E26
Verdi F20–21

▲ An opera rehearsal 150 years ago. (To save expense, the singers wear ordinary clothes, and a piano replaces the orchestra)

▲ 19th-century opera singers had crowds of fans, just like pop singers today. This cartoon shows the crowds waiting for a glimpse of the famous singer Jenny Lind

▶ Audience and performers at the Covent Garden opera in the 18th century. Not every eye is watching the stage: some people find the audience more interesting

More about
Handel F10
Monteverdi F13
Mozart F14
opera D8–9, D12–17, E17
Orpheus E7
Purcell F15

400 years of opera

Opera began in Italy, at the end of the 16th century. People liked to see well known stories acted and sung to music. For example, the composer Monteverdi set to music the story of Odysseus' homecoming after the Trojan War. He wrote another opera based on the Greek legend of Orpheus.

In the 17th and 18th centuries, opera was mainly an entertainment for rich people. Going to the opera was a grand occasion, and the audience was almost as glittering and finely dressed as the performers on the stage. 17th-century audiences liked stories full of spectacular events: to be a real success, your opera might include a storm at sea, an earthquake, or a town on fire. In the 18th century, two main kinds of opera were popular. The first was called **opera seria** ('serious opera'). It used stories from legend or from history. (Handel, for example, wrote an opera about Julius Caesar; you can see some costume designs for a modern production of it on page D14.) The second was called **opera buffa** ('comic opera'). It was funny, and used specially made-up stories, usually about young lovers, scheming servants, and the foolish masters they outwit.

In the 19th and 20th centuries opera became very popular. Many of the world's finest opera-houses were built at this time. Fast travel (by rail, ocean liner, and in this century by air) meant that opera-singers could easily give performances all over the world. The invention of the gramophone made opera, and opera-singing, available to everyone: boxed sets of opera, today, are among the biggest-selling classical records of all.

▲ The waltz-song from *La Bohème* by Puccini. (You can see his picture, and a scene from the opera, on page D12)

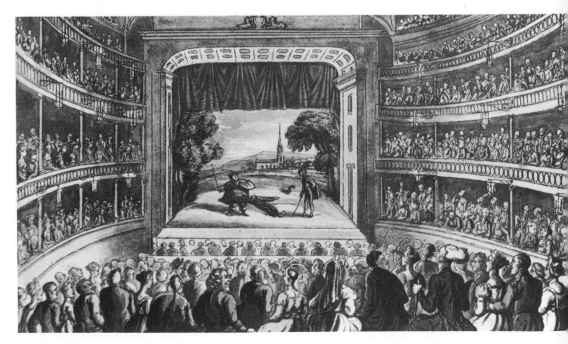

Some operas and their music

Dido and Aeneas by Purcell (first heard in 1689)
This tells the story of how a Roman prince, Aeneas, promised to marry
Dido, queen of Carthage. But the gods ordered him to leave Carthage,
he deserted her, and the unhappy queen killed herself.

🎵 Try listening to Dido's lamenting song after Aeneas has left,
'When I am Laid in Earth'.

▲ The English composer Henry Purcell,
who wrote the music of *Dido and Aeneas*

◄ Dido about to sing 'When I am laid in
earth' from a London performance of
Dido and Aeneas

The Barber of Seville by Rossini (first heard in 1816)
If you want to try comic opera, this is one of the very best. Its story
concerns young lovers, a jealous guardian, a scheming music-teacher,
and the plots and tricks of the barber himself, Figaro.

🎵 Try first the most famous song of all from the opera, *Figaro,
Figaro*, about how busy and important the barber is. Then try
Zitti, zitti, piano, piano ('Quick! Quick! Shh! Shh!'), sung by a group of
people creeping about a dark house at the dead of night.

Don Giovanni by Mozart (first heard in 1787)
Don Giovanni has declared his love to a girl, and then abandoned her.
Her father challenges him to a duel, and Don Giovanni kills him. Then,
later, he mocks the dead man by inviting his statue to come to dinner.
The statue accepts, and drags the wicked Don to his punishment in
Hell. For all its gloomy story, the opera is full of light-hearted, popular
tunes.

🎵 Try the Catalogue Song sung by Don Giovanni's servant
Leporello, and then the serenade *Deh vieni* ('Look down from
your Window'), a beautiful love-song sung by Don Giovanni to mando-
lin accompaniment.

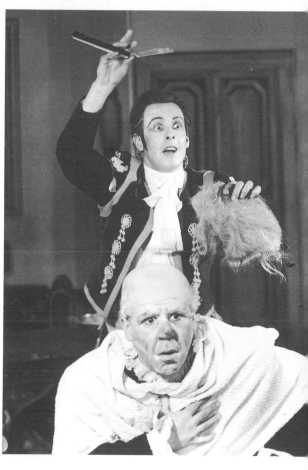

▲ The barber Figaro and his master,
from a London performance of *The
Barber of Seville*

◄ The statue drives the unrepentant
Don Giovanni down to Hell. Leporello
looks on, terrified

D11

▲ The French composer Georges Bizet, who wrote the music of *Carmen*

▶ A fiery Spanish dance from *Carmen*

▲ Three characters from *The Little Sweep:* cruel Black Bob, the chimney sweep, his son Clem and the little sweep, Sam

▲ The Italian composer Giacomo Puccini, who wrote the music of *La Bohème*

▶ Rodolfo comforting Mimi as she lies dying

More about
Britten F28
opera D8–11, 14–15, E17
rehearsing C28–29, D10

Carmen by Bizet (first heard in 1875)

This is one of the most tuneful, dramatic operas ever written – an excellent one to see, if you get the chance. It tells of the love affair between a Spanish soldier called Don José, and the gipsy girl Carmen. Its music is often in Spanish style, with clacking castanets and fiery dance-rhythms.

 Try the Toreador's Song, and the Habanera (a slow, Spanish dance performed by Carmen to attract Don José).

The Little Sweep by Britten (first heard in 1949)

This short opera comes from an entertainment called *Let's make an Opera*, written especially for children. As well as soloists and chorus, it has songs for the audience to join in.

La Bohème by Puccini (first heard in 1896)

The story tells of a group of poor writers and artists in Paris, and of the tragic love affair between a painter called Rodolfo and Mimi, a beautiful girl dying of consumption (a lung disease). The tunes and the emotion of the music make *La Bohème* one of the most enjoyable operas there is. Like *Carmen*, this is one to see if you get the chance.

Try listening to the love duet (it begins *'Che gelida manina'*, 'Your little hand is frozen'), and to the lively waltz-song sung by Mimi's friend Musetta. You can find the music on page D10.

How an opera is made

The words of an opera are called the **libretto** (lib-RET-oh, an Italian word meaning 'little book'). The person who writes them is called the **librettist**. Usually he is a different person from the composer, who writes the music. But some composers (for example Wagner) have written their own librettos.

When librettist and composer set to work, they first choose a story for the opera. It can be a brand-new story, specially invented, or a new telling of an old story. Sometimes the same stories have been used over and over again, by many different composers. There are, for example, over 50 operas based on Shakespeare's play *Macbeth*.

Most operas last for about two to four hours. Usually, like plays, they are divided into **acts** (that is, long sections lasting up to an hour each). A one-act opera, as you would expect from its name, is shorter than usual, and two or more can be performed in the same evening.

When words and music are written, the opera is handed over to the performers. Now a large number of people set to work. First, there is the **conductor**, and his assistant the **répétiteur** (ray-pet-ee-TUR) or coach, who trains the singers and plays the piano for rehearsals. They work with the **singers** and the **orchestra**, helping them to learn the music. The **producer** looks after the singers' acting, and arranges all their movements on the stage.

▲ This unusual and beautiful opera programme was printed on silk for a gala performance before the King of England and the President of France in 1903

▼ The producer John Schlesinger (on the right) rehearses hand movements with a leading lady, while another singer looks on. Opposite you can see the same singer, the Spanish tenor Placido Domingo, in a performance of *La Bohème*

▶ The 19th-century Italian opera composer Donizetti coaching a group of singers

▼ The American conductor Lorin Maazel rehearsing the opera orchestra

▲ This scene from Handel's *Julius Caesar* shows the rich costumes worn by Queen Cleopatra and foolish King Ptolemy. On the right is the designer's original drawing, showing what Cleopatra's costume should be like. You can see how exactly the wardrobe department has followed his design

While rehearsals are going on, the **designer** plans the scenery and costumes. He takes them to the **workshop** (for scenery) and the **wardrobe department** (for costumes), and sees that they are properly made. The **props manager** looks after things like swords, purses, letters, drinking cups, jewels – anything that the singers must use on the stage. The **lighting engineer** plans the lighting for the production. The **front-of-house manager** sees that advertisements are sent out, and that tickets and programmes are printed.

On the first night, the opera is performed for the first time before an audience. On show are the singers, the orchestra, and the conductor, perhaps 100–150 people. But behind the scenes, backing them up, there is an unseen team, often the same size or bigger. Their efforts are just as important to the success of the show we see.

▲ Props: swords and pikes for a battle scene

▶ Wardrobe department: making wigs

D14

▲ Painting the scenery

◄ The stage manager, who is in charge of everything behind the scenes, at his control board

◄ In Wagner's opera *The Rhine Gold* three singers have to appear to be swimming in the river Rhine. This shows how it was done. (The men were hidden behind scenery painted to look like water)

▲ A poster and a ticket for a performance of Puccini's *La Bohème* at La Scala Theatre, Milan, Italy

Enjoying opera

Operas are usually performed in their own language, and this can make it hard to follow what is going on. You can solve this problem by finding out the story of the opera first. There are books (in the music section of the local library) which give all the best known opera stories. Record-sets of operas usually include a printed libretto, with the original words facing an English translation. It's best to read the words *before* you see or hear the opera.

You may prefer to try a sample first. A good way of doing this is to listen to a **highlights record**. Often the **overture** is recorded separately, too, and will give you a flavour of the way the music sounds (the drawback is, no singing).

If you are a newcomer to opera, we recommend the operas mentioned on pages D11 and D12.

More about
backstage at the ballet D30–32
listening to music A9

Operetta

The word **operetta** (op-er-ET-ta) really means 'little opera'. Like an opera, an operetta is a play with music, but part spoken, part sung.

The first operettas were written in 19th-century Paris by Offenbach. In some of his operettas he made fun of the gods and heroes of serious opera: he gave the gods nagging wives, for example, or made them go to work by bus. His operettas were full of hit songs and colourful dances – ideas followed by later composers too. At the end of the 19th century, operetta was popular in Vienna, Austria. Two famous composers there were Johann Strauss and Franz Lehár (whose *The Merry Widow* is one of the best loved operettas ever written).

The best known English operettas are by Gilbert and Sullivan (Gilbert wrote the words; Sullivan wrote the music). You may have heard of *The Mikado, The Pirates of Penzance*, or *The Yeomen of the Guard*. Gilbert and Sullivan wrote at the end of the 19th century; their operettas are still favourites in theatres, schools, and Gilbert and Sullivan Societies today.

The most famous operetta composer in the USA, at the beginning of this century, was Sigmund Romberg. (He wrote *The Desert Song* and *The Student Prince*, two of the most popular operettas ever composed.) As the 20th century went on, composers used some of the ideas of operetta in new forms like the **musical** and **rock opera**.

Some famous operettas

The Merry Widow by Lehár (first heard in 1905)
The Prime Minister of a poor country wants to keep a rich widow (and her money) from emigrating. The only way to do it is to marry her off. He chooses a husband for her, and after much confusion (they pretend they don't want to get married, even though they do), they finally marry, and everyone lives happily ever after.

Try the famous song 'Vilia, Oh Vilia', and the Merry Widow Waltz.

▲ The French composer of operettas, Jacques Offenbach

▲ A scene from the rock opera *Evita* which is set in Argentina, South America. The music is by Andrew Lloyd Webber and the words by Tim Rice

▶ A lively scene from *The Merry Widow*

◄ Koko, his ugly bride-to-be Katisha, and two servant girls from *The Mikado*

▼ The music of *The Mikado* was so popular that it was arranged for dancing. This is the cover of *The Mikado Valse* which was based on tunes from the opera

The Mikado by Gilbert and Sullivan (first heard in 1885)

The story takes place in Japan. A penniless young musician, Nanki-poo, is in love with beautiful Yum-Yum – but she is due to marry Ko-Ko, the Lord High Executioner. Even worse, the Mikado (the cruel prince) has ordered that there must be an execution soon, or there will be trouble – and Nanki-Poo is chosen as the volunteer. Things get even more confused; but in the end Nanki-Poo turns out to be the Mikado's long-lost son, and his marriage with Yum-Yum goes ahead. (Ko-Ko gets to marry someone else: an ugly, elderly lady called Katisha.)

 If you want to hear a complete operetta, this is a good one to try. Its well known songs include 'Three Little Maids from School,' 'A Wandering Minstrel I', and Ko-Ko's sad song 'On a Tree by a River' (or 'Tit-willow, Tit-willow, Tit-willow').

Orpheus in the Underworld by Offenbach (first heard in 1858)

This story is basically the Greek legend of Orpheus. But in Offenbach's version Orpheus is a violin teacher whose wife hates the horrible noises he and his pupils make.

For listening, try the Cancan (a dance where the dancers bend double, and flutter layers of frilly, lacy knickers at the audience – very shocking for the first audience in 1858), and the beautiful song 'When I was King of the Boeotians'.

Die Fledermaus by Johann Strauss ('The Bat', first heard in 1876)

This operetta has a complicated story about a man who should be spending eight days in jail for insulting a policeman, but goes instead to a fancy-dress ball, where he meets his own disguised wife, and falls in love with her. The story is absurd, really just an excuse for waltzes and beautiful songs.

Try the whole of Act Two (the ballroom scene), which contains the operetta's most famous tunes.

▲ The ballroom scene from *Die Fledermaus*

More about
musicals B19, D23–25
Orpheus E7
rock opera B19
Strauss D20

These Stone Age dancers (and the musicians clapping their hands to give a beat) are performing to bring good luck to a hunt

Dancing

Some dance fashions

There has never been a time without dancing. People dance religious dances to please the gods. They dance good luck dances at weddings, fairs, and feasts; war-dances, peace-dances, dances of triumph and joy. Nowadays, dancing can even be prescribed by doctors as exercise.

But most of all, people dance for pleasure. In houses and palaces, village squares and halls, dancing has always been a favourite pastime, the centre of many people's social life.

Each country, and each century, has its own special dances. In the early 18th century, for example, there was a fashionable dance called the **hornpipe**, an imitation of the way people thought sailors danced on board ship. A later craze, one your parents or grandparents may remember, was the **twist**. This was invented in 1959, and swept the world in the next few years.

But some dances do remain popular long after people have forgotten how they began. Sometimes the dance is remembered because of the enjoyable music composers wrote for it. The **minuet** (min-you-ET), for example, was a dance of the 16th and 17th centuries. It became fashionable in the first half of the 18th century; dozens of composers wrote minuets, some for dance use, some for listening. The minuet became a standard part of large-scale concert music like symphonies. (If you want to hear what minuet-music is like, listen to Mozart's 12 Minuets K585, or to the minuets from Handel's *Water Music*.)

A later dance, even more popular, was the **waltz** (wolts). This began in the last part of the 18th century, and was a popular dance for nearly 200 years.

◀ Sailors dancing a hornpipe

▼ Dancing the Landler (an ancestor of the waltz) in 18th-century Austria

▼ Maori dancers from New Zealand

▲ The polka. The dancers hold each other close; some of the spectators disapprove

▶ The gentlemen ask the lady to dance with them later in the evening. She writes their names down on a special dance-card

▲ A grand ball in the 18th century. You can see how the dancers' clothes make it necessary for them to dance apart from one another

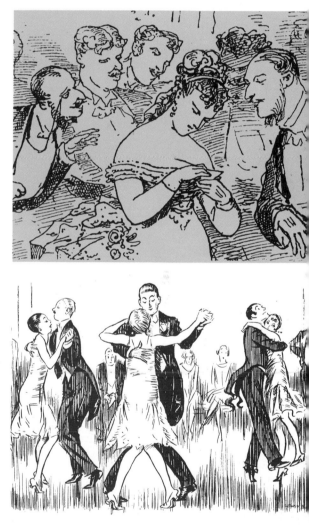

▲ Dancing the charleston: the couples are in step but hardly holding one another closely (except for the couple on the right)

Hand in hand or cheek to cheek?

Until the end of the 18th century, dancers moved in groups, or in long lines. There was very little 'body-contact', with one dancer holding another close. (This was partly because people disapproved of it in public, and partly because fashionable clothes – the wide skirts of the women and swords and ruffs of the men – made it awkward in any case.) The lines of dancers moved in and out, backwards and forwards, swayed, bowed, and curtseyed as the dance went on. This kind of dancing still survives in **country dancing** today, and in party-dances like *Oranges and Lemons* (where two dancers hold hands high in an arch, through which the line of dancers moves).

By the 19th century, a new kind of dancing had become popular in Europe. Instead of the couples dancing in groups or lines, they danced separately – and in some dances (like polkas and waltzes) they held each other closer, too. Some people were shocked by this at first; but it soon became usual. At first, people held each other at arm's length; but gradually this also changed. In the 1930s, for example, couples danced 'cheek to cheek', as the famous dancer Fred Astaire put it in a popular song.

When a couple dances, the skill is often in matching each other's steps exactly, so that the two dancers move together, almost as one. You can see this clearly, nowadays, in **old time dancing**, in the waltz and foxtrot especially. In some 20th-century dances, like **charleston** or **rock 'n' roll**, the dancers move separately, in step with each other but not touching. In a few modern dances (like **disco**) you can dance by yourself, without a partner at all.

More about
folk dancing B2–4, B7–11
dances of the past B15–19,
    D20–21, E6, E11
rock 'n' roll B24

Some favourite dances of the past

15th century

Tordion A fast-moving dance, where lines of dancers, holding hands, move in and out in turning, twisting patterns.

Bransle (pronounced 'brawl') A swaying dance, with the whole line of dancers moving from side to side like a pendulum.

▲ Bransle

16th century

Pavan A slow dance, where the couples step forward in a stately line. It is a dance for showing off rich clothes and graceful movement (originally it was supposed to imitate the movements of a peacock).

Galliard A fast dance for the man. While the woman stands still, or takes small steps to left or right, the man leaps, twists, and bows.

17th and 18th centuries

Minuet A stately dance, with the couples moving in graceful figures round the room.

Cotillion A fashionable version of a country dance, very like our country dancing today. Groups of dancers moved in patterns and lines, in and out, bowing, curtseying, and holding hands.

▲ Pavan   ▶ Minuet

The Strauss family and the waltz

The most famous waltz-music of all was written in the 19th century by the Strauss (Strowss) family of Vienna, Austria. They wrote other kinds of music too (marches, polkas and operettas). But they specialized in the waltz business: as well as composing the music, they published it themselves, conducted it, and played for dances. The best of all their waltzes are those written by Johann Strauss the Elder (1804–49), and his son Johann Strauss the Younger (1825–99). Between them they wrote over 600 waltzes.

Try *The Blue Danube, Artist's Life,* or *Tales from the Vienna Woods.*

◀ Waltz

▼ Polka

19th century

Polka A fast dance, where the couples link arms and skip round the room, almost in imitation of trotting horses.

Waltz A swirling, swaying dance. As well as moving round the room, the couples turn slow circles, like the eddies of a whirlpool.

20th century

Foxtrot A high-stepping, whirling dance, fast or slow, with twirling movements of the feet.

Tango A slow, Spanish-style dance, where the dancers arch their necks and prance or sidle across the room, holding arms and bodies stiff. The rhythm is ♩. ♪♩ ♩: it fits the words 'Look! I'm dancing.'

Rock 'n' roll Rock 'n' roll is really the name of the music. When you dance to it, you are **jiving** or **rocking**. It uses rhythmic hip-twisting, bending the body backwards, and swirling the partners round like catherine wheels.

Formation dancing

In modern dance-halls and ballrooms, you often see **formation dancing**. This is done by a group of people called a **formation team**. The team moves in patterns across the floor, like soldiers drilling or ballet dancers, except that they are using dance-movements. They learn and practise special steps and patterns (called 'routines'), and wear colourful costumes. For people watching, the pleasure is partly in seeing the skill of each individual dancer, and partly the kaleidoscope of colour and movement the whole group makes.

▲ Tango

◀ Formation dancing on the BBC television programme *Come dancing*

More about
dances D18–19, E6
Johann Strauss D17

Stage and television

When you see a variety show, look to see what part the dancers play. Often, they form a kind of moving background to a solo singer. Usually they dance one 'number' by themselves. For the last 100 years, show-girls have been popular in the theatre. They wear identical costumes (like gorgeous uniforms), and dance the same steps in a well-drilled line. They often specialize in tap-dancing, and in high-kicks (kicking your heel as high as your forehead – not easy, in time to the music and all the other girls). Nowadays, on television, you are more likely to see dancers in smaller groups (half a dozen or so). They dance to pop music, and often have names as fanciful as any pop group – *Pan's People*, *New Edition*, *Hot Gossip*, and even *Legs and Co*.

▼ The Tiller girls: famous show-girls from television's *Sunday Night at the London Palladium*

▲ Disco dancers on television

▼ Dancers backing a solo singer on television

Dance films

Ever since sound films began, **dance musicals** have been popular. Their stories are usually cheerful and romantic, and they are filled with songs and dancing.

There are two main kinds of dance musicals. The first uses large groups of dancers. They form into complicated shapes and patterns (like butterflies' wings, flower-petals, catherine-wheels, even maps and flags). The camera often films them from the studio roof, high overhead, so that the patterns can be clearly seen. Some of these films are truly spectacular: in *Flying down to Rio*, for example, dozens of girls tap-dance on the wings of (real) flying planes, high in the air (they were held on with wires and straps); in *Gold Diggers of 1933* there is a living pyramid of dancers on wooden frames 15 metres high.

▲ Gene Kelly in the musical film *Singin' in the Rain.* (You can see another picture from the film on page D24)

◀ Dancers with violins from *Gold Diggers of 1933.* When viewed from above, they look like flower petals

The other kind of dance musical is built round the talents of a single dancing star. The most famous were Gene Kelly and Fred Astaire (whose partner, in some of his best films, was Ginger Rogers). Stars in these films perform in a particularly athletic, gymnastic way, a mixture of dancing, ballet, and acrobatics. They are also expert at **tap-dancing**. For this, you fasten small metal discs (called 'taps') to the underneath of your shoes. When you dance, the taps click on the floor to the beat of the music.

▲ John Travolta starring in *Saturday Night Fever,* a film about a young man who finds success on the dance floor. (For more about John Travolta see page D25)

◀ Fred Astaire and Ginger Rogers tap-dancing

More about
musicals B19, B27, D24–25
dancers D30–31

Some famous film musicals

See them (on television or in the cinema) if you get the chance.

Forty-second Street (1933)

One of the best of the 'group' kind of musical. There are stars who sing and dance. But the most spectacular moments use groups of over 100 dancers, tap-dancing, whirling in waltzes and charlestons, and making huge, living patterns for the overhead camera.

▶ A dance from *Forty-second Street,* showing how the film's scenery looked like jazzy New York, as if all the skyscrapers had come to join the dance

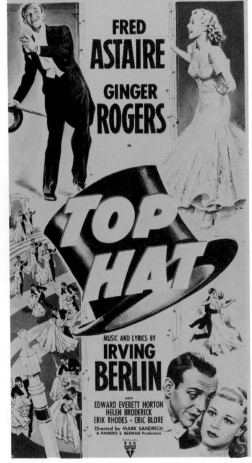

▲ A cinema poster advertising *Top Hat*

Top Hat (1935)

One of the favourite Fred Astaire musicals. He dances on his own (tap and acrobatic), and also with his partner Ginger Rogers, in the kind of ballroom dancing everyone in the world dances – in their dreams. This was one of the first musicals where the dances are not just a kind of added decoration. Instead, they are fitted properly into the story, and carry it along.

*Singin' in the Rain (1952)

This is a comedy about the 'backstage' problems of making the first-ever sound films. Gene Kelly stars, and his singing and dancing (not always in the rain) is some of the best he ever did. Everything about the film is splendid: look out for the extraordinary, acrobatic song-and-dance number 'Make 'em Laugh.'

▶ *Singin' in the Rain*

*The King and I (1956)

The story tells of an English lady who went to teach the 50 children of the King of Siam, and fell in love with him. The music and dancing are partly Western, partly in a colourful, Far Eastern style.

▲ *The King and I,* set in Siam. Here the king tells the English teacher that she must do exactly as he does

*West Side Story (1961)

The story is about two young lovers, on opposite sides in a gang-war in New York. It is a modern version of Shakespeare's *Romeo and Juliet*. The dancing, a mixture of ballet and acrobatics, is some of the best 'group' dancing ever seen on film.

▲ *West Side Story,* set in New York, with music by Leonard Bernstein

◀ *Grease,* starring John Travolta and Olivia Newton-John

Grease (1978)

The story tells of the life and love-affairs of a group of American high-school students in the 1950s, when rock 'n' roll first began. Good group-dancing, splendid singing (from Olivia Newton-John), and some fine dancing-displays from John Travolta.

*If you don't know where to start, start here.

More about
musicals B19, B27, D22–23
Romeo and Juliet E24

Ballet

There are two kinds of ballet (pronounced BAL-lay in Britain, and bal-LAY in the USA). The first kind (sometimes called **story ballet**) is like a play, with dancers instead of actors, and movement instead of words. The second kind (sometimes called **abstract ballet**) has no story. It concentrates on the movements of the dancers, on dance alone, dance for its own sake.

The idea of telling a story in dance before an audience is very old. Though it wasn't called ballet until the 15th century, a form of organized dancing was popular in Egypt 5000 years ago, and also in Greece and Rome. People often hired professional dancers to give a private show.

In the Middle Ages, a dance entertainment was popular with kings and queens. Often a court had its own dance company, who put on shows to entertain the king and his guests, and for special occasions like coronations or royal weddings. The stories were often based on myths or legends: the Labours of Hercules, for example, or the story of Orpheus.

Ballet dancing is tiring, and hard. The movements are as difficult as gymnastics, and you have to make them look easy and graceful, as well as fitting them to the music. For this reason, ballet has usually been a job for professional dancers, after years of training. There have been very few amateurs (people doing it just for fun, and not for a living). Two of the most famous were the rulers of countries: the Roman emperor Nero, and King Louis XIV of France. They loved ballet, were expert dancers, and often performed in ballets specially invented for the court.

▲ A statuette of a ballet dancer from Ancient Egypt

Mime

In a spoken play, we know what characters are thinking and feeling because of the words they use. In many ballets, **mime** is used instead of words. The dancers use hand-movements to tell us their emotions. The idea of mime was invented in ancient Greece, and some of the modern mime-movements have stayed exactly the same. These drawings show some of the commonest – some are very like things people do in everyday life.

▲ This dancer is saying 'I (1) love (2) you (3) and will *never* (4) allow any harm to come (5) to you (6)'

▶ Here the young man in *The Rake's Progress* is being told he should get married

▲ This dancer is using mime to say she promises to obey (in the ballet *The Taming of the Shrew* based on Shakespeare's play)

◄ In 1393 some ballet dancers dressed as devils in spiky, woollen costumes, and performed for a wedding. The costumes, unluckily, caught fire, and two of the dancers were burned to death

▲ King Louis XIV of France in ballet costume as the Sun King

The stories of ballet

Many ballet stories are based on folk tales or fairy tales. Good examples are *Cinderella*, complete with glass slipper and fairy godmother, and *The Firebird*, with its wicked wizard and magic firebird. Other ballets tell stories we know in other forms: *Romeo and Juliet*, for example, is based on Shakespeare's play.

Often, ballet stories include celebrations: weddings, coronations, parties, and balls. This gives the dancers a chance to perform what are called **divertissements** (dee-ver-TEESS-mong). A *divertissement* (or 'diversion') is a group of unconnected dances (waltzes, country dances, minuets, and so on) slipped into the story of the ballet. Famous ballets with *divertissements* include *Giselle* (with a set of country dances) and *The Nutcracker* (with a set of dances from different countries). You can read their stories on the next two pages.

▼ A modern ballet: a scene from Stravinsky's *The Rite of Spring.* (You can read more about it on page E30 of *The Story of Music*)

▶ The Ugly Sisters at the ball (from *Cinderella*). The sisters are played by two male dancers

More about
ballet D28–32
Romeo and Juliet E24
The Nutcracker D29
The Rite of Spring E30

Three ballets and their music

Giselle by Adam (first danced in 1841)
Giselle is a young village girl. She is in love with a boy called Loys, not knowing that he is really Prince Albrecht in disguise. The villagers hold a feast, and Giselle is crowned Queen of the Grape Harvest. But after the dancing, she finds out that Loys is really a prince, and that she can never marry him. In despair, she kills herself with his sword.

Later, Albrecht comes to her tomb in the forest, to beg her to forgive him. Giselle's spirit has been taken to join the Wilis. Any living man who sees the Wilis must dance and dance until he dies. But Giselle forgives Albrecht, and takes pity on him. She dances instead of him. The dawn comes, the power of the Wilis is broken, and Albrecht's life is saved.

▲ *Coppélia:* Swanhilda, dressed as Coppélia, and Dr. Coppélius inside the toyshop (from Act Two)

▼ *Coppélia:* the wedding dance from the last act

Coppélia by Delibes (first danced in 1870)
In the window of Dr Coppélius's toy-shop, a beautiful girl sits reading. The village boys, not realizing she is really a life-size doll, flirt with her and try to make her smile at them. The biggest flirt of all is Frans. His fiancée, Swanhilda, is angry with him. The villagers dance to celebrate the Feast of Marriages, but the lovers quarrel and part.

That night, Swanhilda and her friends steal the key of Dr Coppélius' shop, and creep inside. They discover that Coppélia is really a doll, not the old man's daughter at all. Then they hear Frans outside, fetching a ladder to visit Coppélia. Dr. Coppélius comes in, and the girls hide. Frans climbs in, and Dr. Coppélius grabs him and imprisons him. He wants to steal Frans' life and give it to Coppélia. The doll comes to life. But it behaves strangely, upsetting everything in the shop and refusing to obey Coppélius. He doesn't realize that Swanhilda has dressed in the doll's clothes and taken its place. At last Swanhilda rescues Frans, and they escape. Coppélius is left with the real Coppélia, a lifeless doll. The ballet ends with dancing to celebrate the wedding of Frans and Swanhilda.

Giselle: Giselle and the Princess at the feast of the Grape Harvest. Giselle is in despair at hearing of the princess's engagement to Albrecht

The Nutcracker: Clara, asleep, dreams she is defending her nutcracker against some mice. The old man is her godfather who gave her the nutcracker

The Nutcracker: the prince takes Clara on a journey to Russia

The Nutcracker by Tchaikovsky (first danced in 1892)

Clara, a little girl, is given a Nutcracker doll as a Christmas present. After a Christmas party she falls asleep. The rest of the ballet takes place in her dream. The Nutcracker doll leads an army of toy soldiers against some enemy mice. Clara saves the doll's life, and he turns into a handsome prince. He takes her on a magic journey, through a forest of dancing snowflakes. They come to the Kingdom of Sweets, and are welcomed by its queen, the Sugar Plum Fairy. She gives a party, with dancers from Spain, Arabia, China, and Russia. The ballet ends with a Flower Waltz, danced by everyone on stage.

Try to see the ballets in the theatre if you can.

 For listening, try the Suites made from each of them. The *Nutcracker Suite* is a good one to hear first.

More about
Coppélia D30–31
Tchaikovsky F19

▲ The designer of the ballet *Court of Love,* written for Queen Elizabeth II's jubilee in 1977, with a model of the scenery

▼ Frans, in the ballet *Coppélia*. On the right are the designer's original drawings of his costume

How a ballet is made

A new ballet usually starts with the **choreographer** (kor-ee-OG-ra-pher). He is the man who invents the dance-movements, and teaches them to the dancers. When he begins a new ballet, he looks for a story that can be told through music and dance. The audience must be able to follow it without the need of words.

Next he chooses the music. Sometimes ballets are arranged to music that exists already: symphonies, concertos, suites, and other pieces from the concert-hall. But often the ballet company asks a **composer** to write music especially for a new ballet. Whether it is specially written or not, the music must be suitable for dancing, and fit the mood and style of the story.

The next member of the team is the **designer**. His job is to create scenery and costumes. Ballet is meant to please the eye as well as the ear, and the way it looks is very important. Often the scenery and costumes are very lavish and colourful. The stage, with the dancers on it, is like a beautiful colour picture come to life.

Next, while the scenery is built and the costumes made, the choreographer teaches the ballet to the **dancers**. They learn all the steps and mime-movements by heart, just as actors learn the words and movements of a play. While they practise, the music is played for them by a special pianist called a **répétiteur**.

At last everything is ready. The dancers know their parts, the scenery is built and the costumes made. The orchestra have practised the music, programmes have been printed and tickets sold. While the dancers are made up, and take their places on stage, the audience gathers in its seats. The conductor comes in; the theatre lights go down; the music starts and the ballet begins.

◄ Rehearsing a scene from *Coppélia.* The dancers are playing Swanhilda and her friends, tiptoeing into Dr. Coppélius' workshop

▼ The choreographer teaches the movements of a new ballet step by step. Here he is working with his star dancer

▲ Composer (with beard), choreographer (scratching head) and two dancers resting at a rehearsal

◄ Putting on stage make-up before the show. What sort of part do you think this dancer is going to play?

More about
backstage at the opera D14–15
ballet D26–9, D32
Coppélia D28

Writing a ballet down

The music and story of a ballet can easily be written down, to pass on to other performers. But how do you write down the movements?

At first, there was no exact way. Dancers remembered the movements they had been taught, and taught them to other dancers by heart. This is still the main method used today. But there is also a form of picture-writing, called **dance notation**. You write it under the music, to show which movements you want the dancers to perform. Once your notation is finished, it can be copied and used by dancers everywhere.

In the pictures on this page, you can see five basic ballet positions, and how one particular movement (from *Cinderella*) would be written out in dance notation.

▼ Dancers in the five basic ballet positions

top of head				
shoulders				
waist				
knees				
feet				

▲ How ballet notation works

| Hands and feet in front of the body

— Hands and feet level with the body

● Hands and feet behind the body

† Elbows and knees bent in front of the body

✚ Elbows and knees bent level with the body

✖ Elbows and knees bent behind the body

More about
writing music down G2–10

◄ A moment from the ballet *Cinderella*. You can see below how it is written down in dance notation

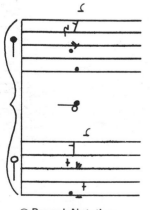

© Benesh Notation

Medieval dancers accompanied by a flute player and drummer

Music through the Ages

buildings · instruments

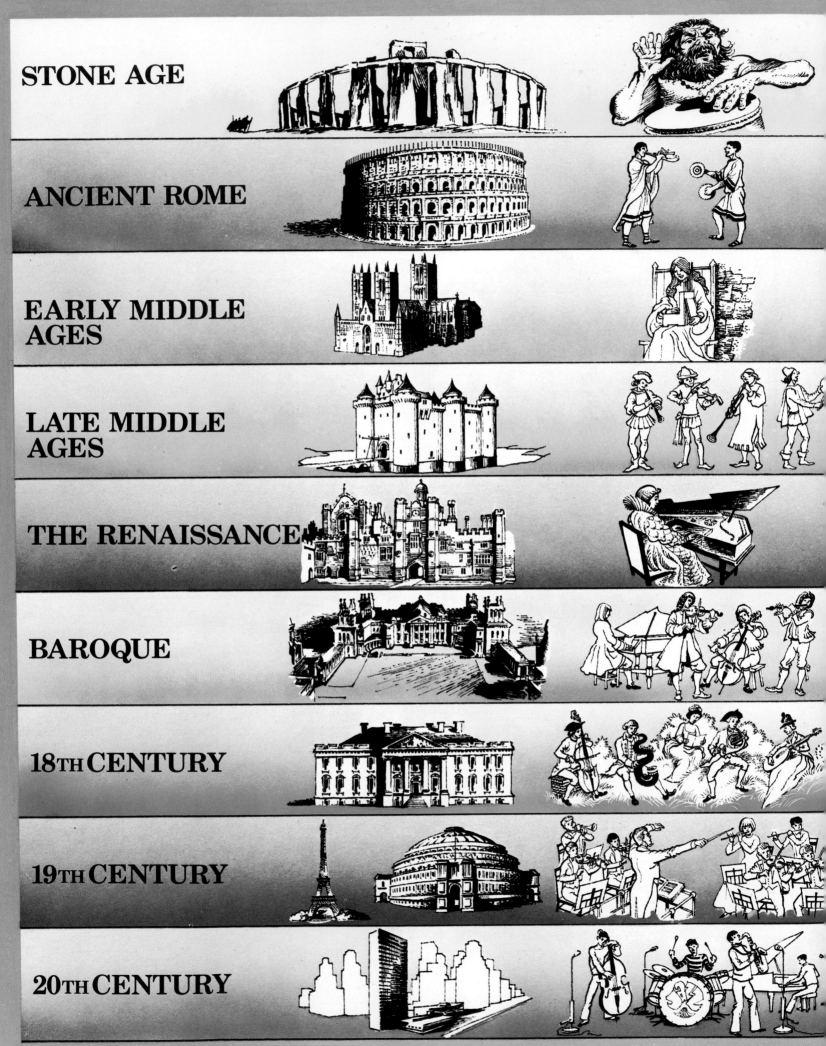

STONE AGE

ANCIENT ROME

EARLY MIDDLE AGES

LATE MIDDLE AGES

THE RENAISSANCE

BAROQUE

18TH CENTURY

19TH CENTURY

20TH CENTURY

dancers   singers   composers

Palestrina
Gabrieli
Byrd

Monteverdi
Lully
Purcell
Couperin

Bach   Mozart
Handel
Vivaldi
Haydn

Beethoven   Wagner   Mahler
Rossini   Verdi   Grieg
Schubert   Strauss   Dvořák
Chopin   Brahms   Tchaikovsky
Schumann   Debussy

Ravel   Copland
Gershwin   Britten
Schoenberg   Shostakovich
Bartók   Bernstein
Stravinsky   Beatles

▲ A cave painting of Stone Age musicians

Ancient music

How do we know?

Our knowledge of Stone Age music comes from cave paintings. These show people singing and clapping more than 10,000 years ago. Later, from the civilizations of Egypt (4000 years ago), of Babylon (3000 years ago) and of Greece (2500 years ago), there are paintings and statues of dancers, and people playing drums, rattles, flutes, trumpets, lyres, and harps. The walls of temples in places as far apart as India and Mexico were covered with decorations: many show musicians performing in honour of the gods. From **art** like this, we know what music-making looked like long ago.

▲ Ancient Egyptian harp player (from a painting on the wall of a pyramid, inside)

▲ Ancient Persian musicians: harp players, flute player and xylophone player

▲ Ancient Greek flute player

Our next knowledge comes from **writing**. People often wrote descriptions of musical scenes: processions, dances, parties, and theatre shows. These tell us how people used music, and what they thought of it.

The most exciting knowledge of all comes from actual **remains**. In many places in the world, people had musical instruments buried in their tombs, to play in the world of the dead. In Egyptian pyramids, in tombs from ancient Persia, Babylon, China, and India, modern archaeologists (the scientists who dig up and study the remains of the past) have found these instruments – some still playable. They give us a few of the actual sounds people heard: a ghostly echo of the music of thousands of years ago.

The sounds of ancient music

Because their music was a kind of magic language, a way of communicating with spirits and demons, Stone Age men probably began by imitating the sounds they thought those spirits made. The first music in the world came from human voices and bodies. As well as shrieking, howling and wailing, people might hiss, click, hum, clap, stamp, and slap their bodies to the beat of the dance.

Soon, however, they must have discovered that they could make music from other things as well. Stones and logs made drums; bowstrings twanged; hollow shells, reeds, and bones whistled or boomed when you blew them. All these sounds were added to the shouting, clapping, and singing, to make the music impress the gods – and the watching humans– even more. Finally, when men discovered metal (in the Bronze Age and Iron Age, about 4000 and 3000 years ago), they made more complicated instruments: trumpets, flutes, metal drums, and gongs. Some were plain, for everyday use; others were decorated with gold and silver, for special occasions. Many of these instruments, and the sounds they made, were not too different from the wind, brass, percussion, and string instruments we use today. You can see some of them in the box on this page.

▲ Ancient Egyptian musicians (from a painting found on a pyramid wall, inside)

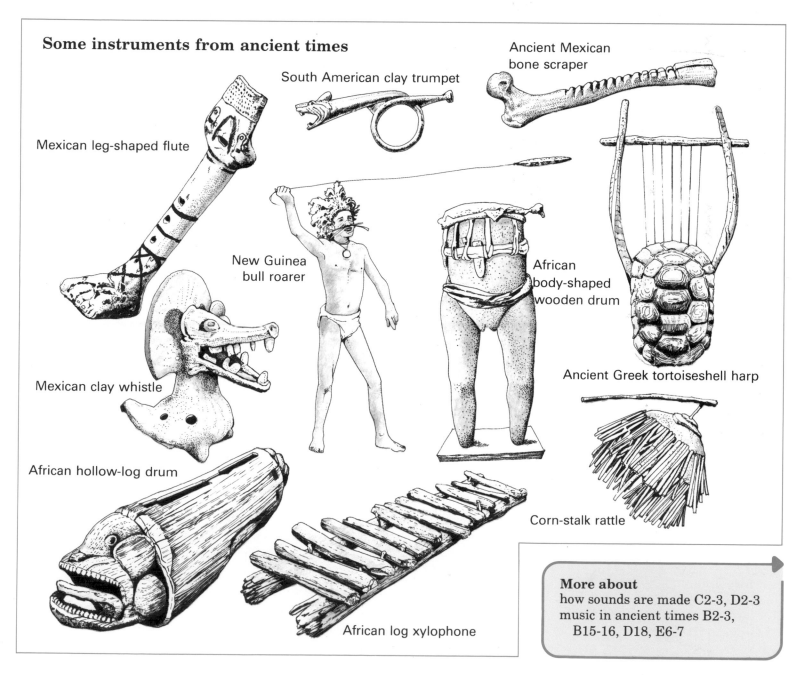

Some instruments from ancient times

Ancient Mexican bone scraper

South American clay trumpet

Mexican leg-shaped flute

New Guinea bull roarer

African body-shaped wooden drum

Ancient Greek tortoiseshell harp

Mexican clay whistle

Corn-stalk rattle

African hollow-log drum

African log xylophone

More about
how sounds are made C2-3, D2-3
music in ancient times B2-3,
B15-16, D18, E6-7

▲ This Peruvian musician is playing the pan-pipes, a modern version of an ancient instrument said to have been invented by the Greek god Pan

Musicians at home and abroad

For early man, music and dancing were two of the most important things in the life of the tribe. They played a part at every gathering. When the people met to worship their gods, to prepare for war or to celebrate a victory, at feasts and festivals of every kind, they made music. On television today, there are sometimes travel programmes about distant tribes. You see them play, dance and sing, often in colourful head-dresses and body-paint. Ancient music-making was probably very much like that.

In Ancient Greece and Rome (about 2500–1500 years ago), music had the same uses (in religion, work, and entertainment) as in earlier times – and as it still does today. Greek and Roman music was often made by slaves: well trained and skilful, the most expensive you could buy. Some musicians were free, and travelled as far afield as traders and soldiers.

The music of ancient Rome

Music was heard in the streets of Rome, more often than in city streets today. Tradesmen sang or whistled to attract buyers; there were processions of people going to the temple for a sacrifice; soldiers or sometimes gladiators sang as they marched; actors played to draw a crowd.

At home, wealthy men sometimes trained their slaves – hairdressers, waiters, cleaners – to sing as they worked. There were singers and dancers to provide entertainment, too. Ordinary people might go out to a café or bar, and find musical entertainment there. You could hire a flute-girl or dancer in the market-place, to come to your house and perform for the evening, just for you, your family and your friends.

More about
music in ancient times B2-3, B15-16, E4-5
Orpheus D10, D17

▲ A Roman lady learning to play the lyre (from a Roman wall painting)

▲ Dancers, flute player and singer from Ancient Egypt

The Greek legend of Orpheus

Orpheus was the finest singer there had ever been. Whenever he sang, the whole world listened: men, animals, birds, even trees and solid rocks. The gods, too, came down to hear him. Orpheus was their delight, their favourite.

Once day Orpheus's wife Eurydice was bitten by a snake, and died. She went down to the Underworld. Orpheus was in despair. Without Eurydice, he said he would never sing again. So the gods granted him a favour, something they allowed no other living man. He could go down to the Underworld, and sing for the King of the Dead. If he pleased the King, he could take Eurydice back to the Upper World, to live again.

Afraid, Orpheus went down the dark tunnels of the Underworld. He found the King of the Dead, and sang for him. At the sound of his voice, all the ghosts of the Underworld wept. They remembered the joys of the Upper World, the sweetness and pleasure they had left forever. The King granted Orpheus his wish. He could lead Eurydice back to life – but on one condition. Until they reached the Upper World, he was not to look back at her. If he turned round just once, she would be lost forever.

Orpheus led the way, up the dark tunnels. He heard no sound behind him: no footsteps, no breathing. How could he be sure Eurydice was really following him? He endured it till the very gate of the Upper World. Then he could bear it no longer. He turned and looked – and Eurydice disappeared forever.

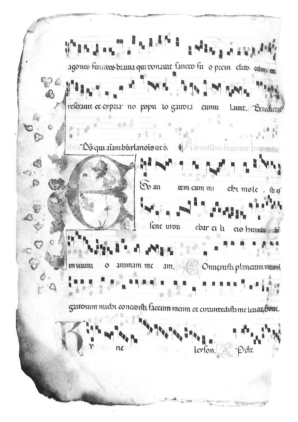

▲ A manuscript of a plainsong chant beautifully copied out by hand

▲ Angel playing the viol (from a stained glass church window)

▶ A group of medieval monks and choirboys chanting

The Middle Ages in Europe (about 400 A.D. – 1450 A.D.)

Christian church music

As Christianity spread across Europe, so did church music. All Christians worshipped the same god, wherever they were. They used the same words, the same church services, and the same sorts of music.

At first, the music was very plain, very simple. The monks and nuns chanted **plainsong**. No instruments were used, and there was only one line of sound. Plainsong is still sometimes used in monasteries and cathedrals today. When you hear monks chanting, in procession or in church, the sound they make is plainsong.

Gradually, the music became more complicated. Instead of a single line of melody, two or more different strands were sung together. Each group of voices (trebles, altos, tenors, basses) had its own strand, and their blending made the music.

Plainsong had been easy for a whole choir to remember and learn by heart, because it had just one line. But it was difficult to remember the new style, because there were several intertwining lines. People began to look for ways of writing it down. A system of lines and notes was invented. At first it was very simple, and gave only a rough guide to what was wanted. But gradually musicians improved it, until it became the system of staves, clefs, and notes we use today. This is how the music of the plainsong chant *Veni creator spiritus* (Come, Holy Ghost) was written in the Middle Ages:

And this is how it would be written today.

(Ve -ni cre – a – tor_ spi -ri – tus)
(Come, Holy Ghost)

◄ An orchestra of angels playing various medieval string and wind instruments

More about
church music D5-7, G13
the Middle Ages B17, D20, E10-11

Some instruments of the Middle Ages

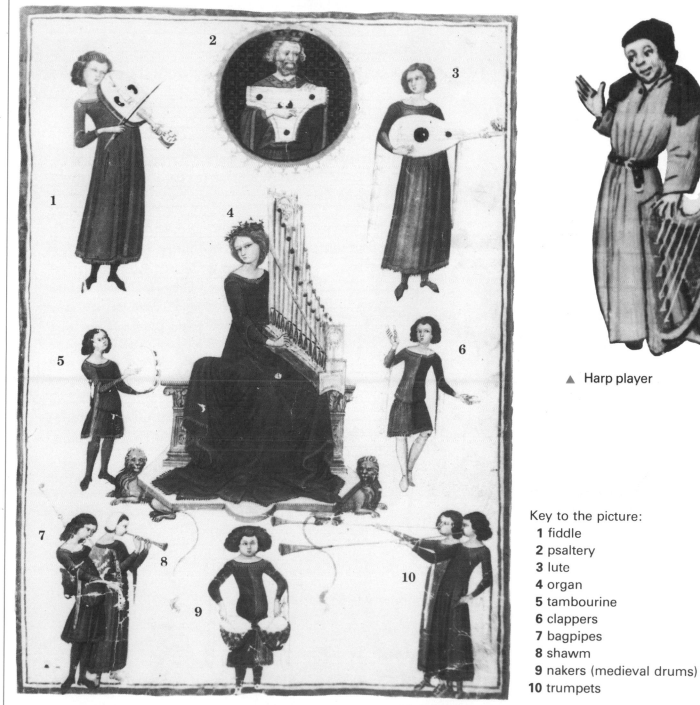

▲ Harp player

Key to the picture:
1 fiddle
2 psaltery
3 lute
4 organ
5 tambourine
6 clappers
7 bagpipes
8 shawm
9 nakers (medieval drums)
10 trumpets

Music for entertainment

As well as in church, music was popular for entertainment. Travelling musicians were welcome everywhere: they brought new tunes and songs, and made a change from the playing of local musicians. Often they had other skills as well, for example dancing, juggling, acrobatics, and telling jokes.

In castles and palaces, rich men had musicians (called 'minstrels') of their own. If you visit an old hall or castle today, you may find a 'minstrels' gallery', a balcony high up in the wall of the main hall. Here minstrels made music to entertain their employer and his guests. One of the songs they might have sung was *Summer is a-coming in*. Here is how it was written down in the Middle Ages:

▲ Three musicians in the minstrels' gallery play for a courtly dance

◄ Minstrel plucking a gittern, the medieval guitar

► A fiddle player

◄ A rebec player

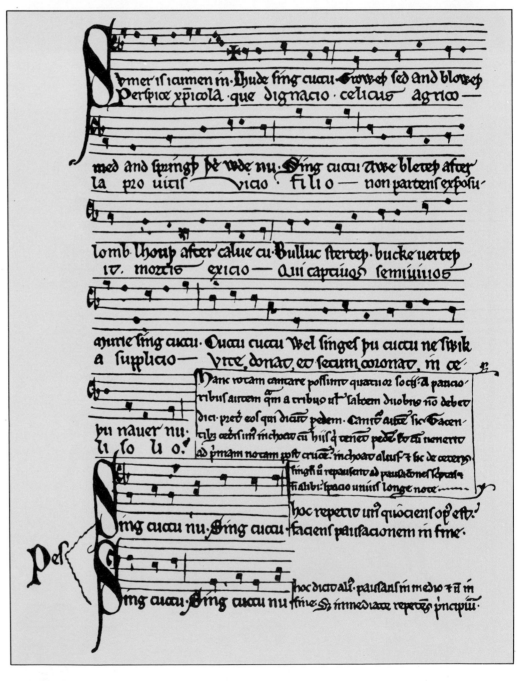

And here is how we write it now.

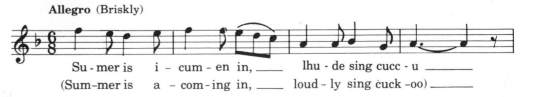

Allegro (Briskly)

Su - mer is   i - cum - en in, ___ lhu - de sing cucc - u
(Sum-mer is   a - com - ing in, ___ loud - ly sing cuck -oo) ___

A rich man and his family enjoy their feast, while the guitarist plays

Music of the Middle Ages

In church you would hear the music of the services. There might be a small band of instruments, and if the church was large and wealthy, perhaps an organ too.

In the village or town square there would often be bagpipers and fiddlers playing for dancing, or just to entertain. They would gather at the local inn, and a crowd would soon come to hear them play.

If the lord of the manor passed by, you might hear ceremonial trumpet-calls or beating drums. If you visited his castle, you might hear fanfares when he came into the room, and his minstrels would sing and play while he ate his meals. This kind of music was called 'table music', and was often made up specially to fit each course. (Fast music, perhaps, for spicy foods; slow music for puddings. What sort of piece would you have to go with roast beef or ice cream nowadays?)

Angels playing a fanfare to announce the coming of Christ

A bagpiper playing for dancing at a village wedding. This painting is by the famous Flemish artist Brueghel

> **More about**
> the Middle Ages B17, D20, E8-9
> entertainers B17, B18, E19, E21

The Renaissance (1450–1600)

What does 'Renaissance' mean?

Renaissance (re-NAY-sons) is a French word, and means 'rebirth'. It is the name given to the 15th and 16th centuries: the time of men like Columbus, Galileo, Shakespeare, and Michelangelo. The people of the Renaissance thought that men of the past had lived in dark times of war, disease and ignorance. Now, they felt, a new age was beginning: mankind was being reborn. Whatever human beings tried to do, they had the knowledge and skills to make a success of it.

Church music

In the Renaissance, many composers wrote their finest music for use in church. In cathedrals and churches today, and in concerts of choral music, their works are still performed. Sometimes you hear voices alone, without instruments, as in masses by Palestrina (1526–1594), or masses and anthems by Byrd (1543–1623). Sometimes the music is a rich blend of voices and instruments, for example in the **motets** and sacred songs of Gabrieli (1555–1612) and Monteverdi (1567–1643).

▲ Galileo, the famous astronomer, explaining his idea that the earth revolves round the sun

▲ Inside St Mark's Cathedral, Venice, Italy. Musicians often played from the galleries high up in each wall

◀ Musicians and listeners in a Renaissance nobleman's home

▲ The composer Palestrina showing one of his books of masses to the Pope

▲ Music-making in the open air: virginals, lute, recorder and viola da gamba (an ancestor of the cello)

Some Renaissance inventions and discoveries

1454 Gutenberg made the first European printed book. (Until then, all books were copied out by hand.)

1477 First rifle.

1489 Plus (+) and minus (−) signs first used in Maths.

1492 Columbus discovered the West Indies. First globe of the earth made. (Until then, most people had believed that the earth was flat.)

1509 Henlein invented the pocket-watch (at first called the 'Nuremberg Egg', because of its shape).

1520 Chocolate and coffee first brought to Europe from South America.

1543 Copernicus proved that the earth moves round the sun. (Until then, people thought that the earth was the centre of the universe, and that all the planets, and the sun, revolved round it.)

1550 First spectacles prescribed for poor sight.

1565 First lead pencils used.

1586 Tobacco and potatoes first brought to Europe from South America (tomatoes followed in 1596).

1609 Galileo perfected the telescope.

More about
choral music D5-7, G13
Monteverdi F13
Renaissance music E14-15

▲ Three musical ladies: one is singing, while the others are playing the flute and lute

▶ Virginals music: the opening of *Giles Farnaby, His Humour*, a piece by the Elizabethan composer Giles Farnaby

▲ Queen Elizabeth I dancing with one of her courtiers

▶ A musical family of the Renaissance: father plays the lute, mother the virginals, while the others (and the dog) listen

More about
Elizabethan music B20, D20
instruments C18

Ladies and gentlemen

Until the Renaissance, many knights and lords believed that nothing mattered except wealth and power. So long as you beat your enemies and made money from your estates, it was no one else's business what sort of man you were.

Renaissance men thought differently. As well as enjoying wealth and power, a true gentleman ought to be a *cultured* man. That is, he should be able to read and write, perhaps dance and paint a little, and certainly take part in conversation about pictures, books and plays.

Above all, a gentleman should be interested in music. This fashion was set by kings and princes. In England, for example, Henry VIII played the recorder and viol, sang, and wrote music. Mary Queen of Scots played the lute, and wrote songs. Elizabeth I played the virginals, and sang.

Where princes led the way, courtiers followed. No gentleman's home was properly furnished without a 'chest' (that is, box) of recorders, consort (or family) of viols, or musicians' gallery. Ladies learned to play the lute and the virginals. People sang **madrigals** (you can read what they are on the opposite page), and danced graceful, courtly dances like the pavan, sarabande and galliard.

Lightly

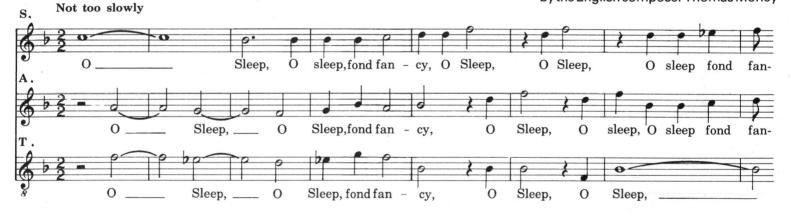

A madrigal-singing party in the open air

Music for the lute, written in *tablature* (see page G10 of *Writing Music*)

Madrigals

For Renaissance ladies and gentleman, **madrigals** were a favourite form of music. They are songs, usually for four, five, or six voices. Sometimes you hear them today performed by choirs, sometimes by groups of solo voices. The words are often about lovers, or nymphs and shepherds. Famous composers of madrigals include Lassus, Monteverdi, and the Englishmen Morley, Wilbye, Farnaby and Weelkes.

The beginning of a favourite Renaissance madrigal *O sleep, fond fancy* by the English composer Thomas Morley

Renaissance music

In village squares and inns you would hear popular songs and dance-tunes; on Sundays and holidays you might take part yourself in round-dances or singing games. In larger churches, as well as the chanting and choir-music of ordinary services, there might be specially grand music for Christmas and Easter: this would be your chance to hear an orchestra, and solo singers, as well as the main church choir.

In towns, you would hear street-traders 'singing their wares'. Each trader had his own little tune (to words like 'Hot pies, hot!', or 'Buy my sweet lavender'); some of them became popular for their own sakes, like the musical jingles of advertisements today. Another common sound in towns and large villages was the music of a troupe of actors, the fanfares, songs, and dances as they performed their plays.

For ladies and gentleman, there were concerts (by groups of recorder players, or viol players, or mixed groups of voices and instruments). They also enjoyed dancing, and many played instruments and sang themselves.

A hurdy-gurdy player at a fair

E15

Baroque music (1600–1750)

What does 'Baroque' mean?

Baroque (ba-ROK) is a word used about buildings. A Baroque building is decorated with twisting, curling patterns, and has carvings and paintings everywhere. Buildings like this were especially popular in the 17th century (300 years ago). To some people, the music of that time also seems to twist and turn, and to be full of decorations and ornaments. So it is called Baroque as well.

▼ Trumpeters and drummers in the coronation procession of King James II of England, 1687

▲ Swirling decoration on a Baroque church in Rome, Italy

▼ A baroque violin with a decorated carved back

Harpsichord and violin

For Baroque musicians, two popular instruments were the **harpsichord** and **violin**. Harpsichords were often made to be beautiful pieces of furniture as well as instruments, and were decorated with carvings and paintings. The string instrument makers of the time were some of the finest there have ever been. Two Italian families in particular, Stradivari and Guarneri, made magnificent instruments still used today. Because of their beautiful sound, Stradivarius (strad-i-VAR-i-us) or Guarnerius (gwar-NAYR-i-us) violins, violas and cellos are still regarded as the best in the world: they are highly prized, rare, and very expensive.

One of the most famous composers of harpsichord music was the Frenchman Couperin (1668–1733). Couperin (KOOP-er-an) liked to give his pieces expressive names, like paintings or poems: 'Bees', 'Butterflies', 'The Nightingale in Love', or 'The Spinning Top'. Here is the opening of one of them, *Le tic-toc-choc*.

Lightly and rhythmically

The greatest violin composer of the time was Vivaldi. He wrote more than 450 concertos, including 200 for violin. The most famous are the group called *The Four Seasons*. In them, the music paints musical pictures of scenes in Spring, Summer, Autumn, and Winter.

Music for the stage

Many Baroque composers wrote music for the stage. As well as operas, ballets, and incidental music for plays, they wrote **masques** (MASKS). A masque is designed to be as lavish and impressive as possible. It is a mixture of speaking and song, rather like a modern musical– and like a musical, it often has dancing in it too. The scenery was usually beautifully painted (sometimes with silver-leaf and gold-leaf decoration as well). Many masques had parts in them for gods and goddesses, who floated overhead on wires, sometimes supported by winged chariots or painted clouds.

Two of the main stage composers of the time were Lully and Purcell. You can read more about them on pages F12 and F15 of *Composers and their Music*.

◀ A stage set for a masque. The actors float overhead on clouds supported by wires

More about
harpsichord C18
violin C12
some baroque composers F2-3,
  F10, F12, F15, F21
church music D5-7, G13

Luther and chorales

In 1517 in Germany, Martin Luther began the religious movement now known as the **Reformation**. He and his followers protested at some of the ideas of the Catholic Church, and so came to be known as Protestants. One of their main changes was to make church services easier to understand. In Catholic churches everything was in Latin; in Protestant churches it was in the people's own language. The words and music of the service were made simpler, so that everyone could join in.

To help in this, Luther used hymns, with tunes the congregation (the worshippers in the church) could sing for themselves. Luther's hymns were called **chorales** (ko-RAHLS). He wrote many tunes himself, and based others on folk tunes. Many chorales are still among the best known of all hymn tunes: for example, *A safe Stronghold our God is still (Ein' feste Burg)*, *O sacred Head sore wounded (Passion Chorale)*, and *Sleepers, wake (Wachet Auf)*.

▶ Luther preaching

◀ The tune of Luther's chorale *Sleepers, Wake*

The 18th century (1700–1800)

Fashions in music

For many rich people 250 years ago, enjoying music was a fashionable thing to do. Sometimes you gave elegant music parties, and invited friends. There would be plenty of food, wine, and talk – and the best music money could buy. You could hire musicians for the day or the evening; but if you were rich and enjoyed music, you would have a band or orchestra of your own.

▲ An outdoor orchestral concert in an 18th-century German town. Light is provided by a half-circle of footmen holding blazing torches. Spectators crowd around — and the luckier ones watch and listen from the upstairs windows of the houses

As well as hearing music at home, you could go out to operas, concerts or dances. At fashionable events like these, the people were putting on a show themselves. They wore their finest clothes, dazzling jewels, and stiff, powdered wigs. Often they played cards, drank coffee, waved to their friends, and gossiped while the musicians played. Once, during a concert in Bath, England, two gentlemen even fought a duel.

The Esterházy family had two palaces. Here is a view of their castle at Eisenstadt, south of Vienna. You can see a picture of their country palace on page F11, *Composers and their Music*

Musicians and their employers

For most 18th-century musicians, the usual way of earning a living was to work for an employer. Sometimes your employer was a church official, and you were paid to provide music for church services. Sometimes he was one of the nobility, a lord or a duke, and you provided music for his own enjoyment, and to entertain his guests at social gatherings.

Usually the system worked well. If you worked for an important church, or for a real music-lover, there was plenty of interesting work to do. At St Thomas's Church, Leipzig, for example, Bach was in charge of everything to do with music: singing, organ-playing, teaching the choirboys, conducting at all the church services, and even looking after the instruments and seeing that the organ was kept in tune. At the palace of Esterháza, where Haydn was musician-in-charge, there was an orchestra, a choir, a wind band, an opera house, and even a puppet theatre. All the musicians at Esterháza (over 100 people) worked for just one man, the prince. They played for dances and banquets, gave opera performances, and put on concerts several times a week. For Haydn, the man in charge, it was an extremely busy, varied life.

Sometimes employers and musicians disagreed. To some employers, the musician was just another servant. If there was a disagreement, he was expected to give in, and do as he was told. Musicians sometimes didn't care for this, and so there were difficulties. Bach, for example, quarrelled with his church employers at Leipzig; Haydn's employer expected him to eat with grooms and footmen; one of Mozart's employers lost his temper, and had him kicked down a flight of stairs.

St Thomas's Church, Leipzig, Germany, in Bach's time

Musicians employed by Frederick the Great, King of Prussia, entertain the court. The King himself is playing the flute

Freelance musicians

If working for an employer was not to your taste, you could work as a **freelance musician** instead. A freelance is someone who works for himself, taking on only the jobs he wants to do. Many musicians worked for the theatre, playing in operas, and providing incidental music for plays. (One of the most famous of all 18th-century composers, Handel, worked in this way.) Others travelled from town to town, playing for dances and entertainments, and putting on concerts.

For a freelance musician, it was important to have generous **patrons**. A patron gave you a **commission**: that is, he asked you to write him a particular piece, and paid you a fee for doing it; or he invited you to his house to give music lessons, or to perform. For musicians like Mozart, who disliked working for full-time employers, patrons were an important way of earning money while keeping your freedom.

▲ Ticket for a concert in 1799, designed by the English painter William Hogarth

Musicians on tour

It was no joke, touring round Europe in the 18th century. Most of the roads had been first built by the Romans, over 1500 years before. They were rough, and full of potholes – and no one owned them, so no one was responsible for repairing them. In wet weather they were muddy, in dry weather full of choking dust. The coaches were draughty and rickety, and went at no more than 10–15 km an hour. The journey was full of risks – getting lost, losing a wheel, crashing and highwaymen.

When you reached journey's end at last, and found somewhere to stay, the work began. Some composers gave concerts, usually of their own music. Others went to the opera-house, to conduct their latest operas. But many visited the houses of rich aristocrats, hoping to interest them in their playing or composing skill.

Another problem for the travelling musician was that many rich music-lovers had bands and orchestras of their own. Sometimes these local musicians welcomed visitors. But they could also be jealous and unhelpful, especially if the visitor was talented.

It was expensive paying for lodgings and hiring concert-halls. But if you were lucky, you could earn a handsome profit. Sometimes you were paid with presents: watches and jewellery – pretty, but not always so useful as hard cash.

▲ Inside a concert-hall: this cartoon shows a singer giving everyone a hard time

Orchestras and symphonies

At the start of the 18th century, although opera-houses, large churches and some rich men's houses had orchestras, there were very few public concerts.

As the century went on, the idea of public concerts grew. Orchestras were formed in many large towns. In them, the players were no longer hired for each performance, a collection of strangers. Instead, they trained together until they became a musical team.

Until this time (perhaps because no one expected to listen to an orchestra playing on its own), the music written for orchestras had been small-scale: mainly divertimentos, serenades and suites. Audiences preferred singers and concerto soloists, and only half listened when the orchestra played by itself. But now, a new kind of orchestral music became common: the **symphony.**

At first, symphonies were short and easy to listen to. But from 1750 onwards, as the idea of orchestral concerts became popular, the symphony became more and more important. Two composers in particular, Haydn (who wrote over 100 symphonies), and Mozart (who wrote over 40), made it into one of the main kinds of music a composer could write.

18th-century music

In the country, music was much as it always had been: fairs, folk songs and folk dances, visiting actors and musicians. A favourite kind of music was the **ballad**. This was a song telling the story of some local piece of news, or of some great event (like a Coronation or a victory in war). Accounts of murders and highwaymen were especially popular. The ballad-singer sang his song, and then sold copies of the words, at a halfpenny or a penny a time.

Many large towns had 'pleasure gardens', parks where you could walk among trees and flowers, listen to music, watch acrobats and theatre shows, dance, eat, and drink. Some (like the Vauxhall Gardens in London) have disappeared under modern buildings, but others (like the Tivoli Gardens in Copenhagen, Denmark) are still there, and are used in the same way today. A popular song of the time was *Rule, Britannia*. You can hear it performed every year on the last night of the Henry Wood Promenade Concerts, London.

▲ Ballad singer

Lively (trumpet) original key: C

When Bri-tain first__ at Heav'n's com-mand,   A -

- rose _____ from out the a – zure main,

◄ An open-air concert in Vauxhall Gardens, London, 1785

More about
18th-century music A13, D18-20, E18-19
some 18th-century composers F2-3, F5, F10-11, F14, F21

Some inventions and discoveries of the 17th and 18th centuries

1607	First known use of dining-fork, in Italy. (Until then, people used their fingers, spoons, or the points of knives.)
1610	Tea first brought to Europe from India.
1628	Harvey explained how the heart pumps blood round the body. (Until then, people thought it stood still, like stagnant water in a pipe.)
1645	First known use of wallpaper (instead of paint, tapestry, or wooden panelling).
1681	First fixed street-lamps in London. (Until then, a **link-boy** walked ahead of you, carrying a lantern.)
1705	Newcomen's steam engine. First use of springs to make carriage-rides less bumpy.
1733	First mechanical weaving-loom (worked by a steam engine).
1768	Cook discovered New Zealand and Australia.
1783	First flight by man (by the Montgolfier brothers, in a hot-air balloon).
1790	Sewing machine invented (at first used only for sewing shoes).
1797	First parachute jump (by Garnerin, from a hot-air balloon).

The 19th century (1800—1900)

Music in the home

At the start of the 19th century, the lives of many people began to change. Newly invented machines, worked by steam power, were changing industry. Instead of goods being produced one at a time by craftsmen, working on their own, they could now be mass-produced in thousands, in factories. Some were luxuries (like silver-plated knives and forks, or fine woven carpets); but there were ordinary household goods as well, things to make life easier or more comfortable – furniture, needles and thread, soap, linoleum. Factory-made goods were often cheap and good, and more people could afford them. For many men and women (especially factory owners in the new, industrial towns), the 19th century was a bustling, prosperous time.

As more people had money to spend, and spare time to fill, they too became interested in 'the arts': books, music, and pictures. Public libraries and public art galleries were opened in the new, thriving towns, and music publishers and instrument-makers began to concentrate on music for the home.

The favourite home instrument was the **piano**. As well as large grands (for concert-halls), all kinds of smaller sizes (suitable for ordinary living-rooms) were mass-produced in piano factories. The most popular kinds were the 'square piano' (the size of a table), and the 'upright piano' (the size of a dresser or large bookcase).

The great thing about a piano is that it is a complete musical instrument on its own. You can play tune and accompaniment yourself, without needing the help of anyone else (as you do with a flute, say, or a trumpet, instruments which can play only one note at a time). The piano is also ideal for playing accompaniments – for other instruments and singers, for dancing, even for poetry readings and party games.

▲ Musical boxes

▲ 19th-century upright piano: a polished, well-made piece of furniture

▶ When every household had a piano, and walls were thin, the musical battle was ready to begin . . .

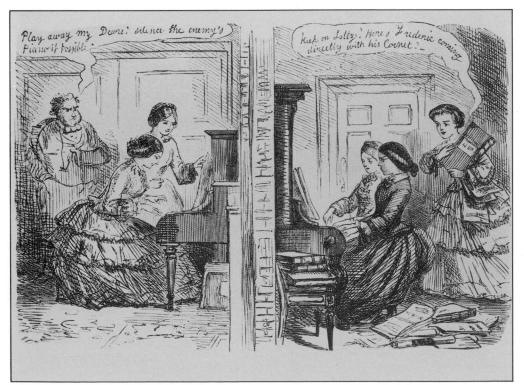

▲ A 19th-century Swiss family relaxing
with music, books and knitting

▲ Covers of the sheet music for two
popular songs

For many 19th-century children (especially girls), learning music
was as much part of growing up as hopscotch or playing with toy
soldiers or dolls. Publishers poured out music of every kind: songs,
dances, piano solos, duets (two players at one keyboard), arrangements of symphonies and overtures, sheets of hymns and patriotic
tunes. No musical home was complete without a box or pile of 'sheet
music' – a few printed sheets at a time, containing one song or a single
piano piece. Sheet music was cheap, and you could quickly build up a
varied collection – rather as people collect pop 'singles' today. One of the
popular hits of the day was *Love's old sweet song*. Ask one of the older
members of your family if they remember it!

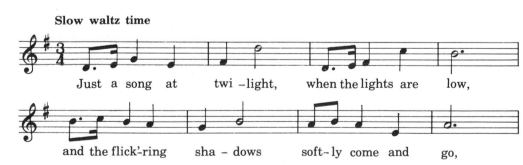

This piece, *Zampa*, was a favourite piece for orchestra.

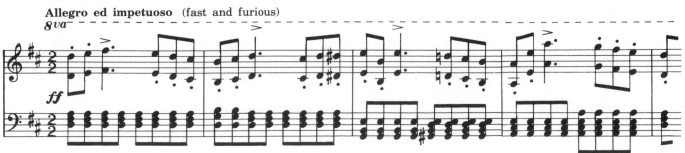

'Romantic' music

▲ A family concert with everyone playing a different instrument. Even in the 19th century such a talented group was rare

Very often, people call 19th-century music **Romantic**. Nowadays, we usually connect the word 'romantic' with love-stories, in films or magazines. But in music, the word means something different.

Until the 19th century, people thought that the main job of music was to please the mind. Just as pictures pleased our sense of sight, or perfume our sense of smell, so music pleased our sense of hearing. But 19th-century people thought that music could also affect our emotions and our feelings. It might make us feel calm or excited, restful, happy, or sad. So, when a composer wrote music, he often intended a particular feeling to be part of it. 'Personal', 'full of emotion' – that's what 'romantic' means.

Many 19th-century composers wrote pieces of music which 'told a story': that is, if you knew the story, you could hear it pictured in the music as the piece was played. There were no words: the music itself told you what was happening. For some pieces, the stories were made up specially. (In Berlioz's *Symphonie Fantastique*, for example, the story behind the music is about a doomed love affair.) For others, the story came from a poem, novel, or play. (You can read about two of the most popular, *Romeo and Juliet* and *Faust,* on these two pages.)

Two stories popular with 19th-century composers

Romeo and Juliet

This story comes from the play by Shakespeare. It is about two rich families, the Capulets and the Montagues. They are at war with one another. Romeo Montague and Juliet Capulet fall in love. They are secretly married. Later, in a fight between Montagues and Capulets, Romeo kills one of the Capulets. He is forced to go into hiding. Meanwhile, Juliet's father, knowing nothing of his daughter's marriage, makes plans for her to marry another man. To prevent this, Juliet drinks a sleeping potion which will make her seem dead. Then, when she has been laid to rest in the church, she will escape and join Romeo. By chance, Romeo comes on her sleeping body. He thinks she is dead, and himself commits suicide. When Juliet wakes up, she finds his body, and kills herself as well. The two lovers are dead; their deaths shame their families into ending the quarrel.

More than 50 19th-century composers wrote operas based on the story of *Romeo and Juliet*. There are also the symphony *Romeo and Juliet* by Berlioz, and the overture *Romeo and Juliet* by Tchaikovsky. The musical *West Side Story* puts the Romeo and Juliet story into a modern setting: the street gangs of New York.

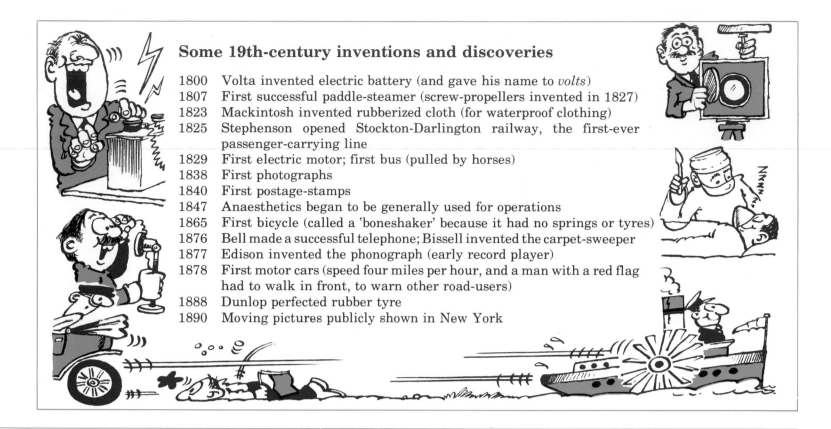

Some 19th-century inventions and discoveries

1800	Volta invented electric battery (and gave his name to *volts*)
1807	First successful paddle-steamer (screw-propellers invented in 1827)
1823	Mackintosh invented rubberized cloth (for waterproof clothing)
1825	Stephenson opened Stockton-Darlington railway, the first-ever passenger-carrying line
1829	First electric motor; first bus (pulled by horses)
1838	First photographs
1840	First postage-stamps
1847	Anaesthetics began to be generally used for operations
1865	First bicycle (called a 'boneshaker' because it had no springs or tyres)
1876	Bell made a successful telephone; Bissell invented the carpet-sweeper
1877	Edison invented the phonograph (early record player)
1878	First motor cars (speed four miles per hour, and a man with a red flag had to walk in front, to warn other road-users)
1888	Dunlop perfected rubber tyre
1890	Moving pictures publicly shown in New York

Faust

This story comes from a play in verse by the German poet Goethe. It tells of Faust, a learned man who lives in the Middle Ages, a time of superstition and black magic. He longs to possess all the knowledge in the world. To test him, God sends the Devil, Mephistopheles, down from Heaven. Mephistopheles charms and delights Faust. He says he will show him all the knowledge in the world – at the risk of Faust's own soul. They make magic spells, and talk with spirits and demons. They sample all the delights and pleasures of the world. But the more Faust learns, the more evil his knowledge seems to him. He even betrays his beloved, Margaret (or Gretchen for short): in despair, she kills their child and is driven mad. Only at the end of his life is Faust saved. He realizes that the knowledge he longed for is worthless, compared with the love of God. Mephistopheles disappears. Faust dies, and his soul is taken up into heaven.

Many composers of the 19th century wrote music based on the story of Faust. Two of the best known pieces are Liszt's *Faust Symphony,* and Gounod's opera *Faust.*

More about
19th-century music A12, A13, D18-19, E22-5, E26-7
Romeo and Juliet D25, D27
some 19th-century composers D20, F5-8, F12, F13, F16-17, F19-27

▲ The virtuoso violinist Paganini

▲ Liszt giving a spectacular display at the keyboard

▲ One of the first London 'promenade concerts' in 1849; they were called promenade concerts because instead of sitting the audience could promenade (that is, walk about)

More about
19th-century music A13, D18-19, D21
piano C19
19th-century piano composers F5, F8, F12-13, F17

Concerts

As the interest in music spread, more and more people began to enjoy going out to **concerts**. Sometimes there were concerts of local talent: singers and players from your own area grouped together to hire a hall, and play for their family and friends. (The composer Brahms made his first public appearance at one such concert, aged 15, playing one of his own piano pieces.)

At another kind of concert, instead of local performers, you went to hear star performers, or **virtuosos**, play or sing. Usually their music was spectacular, and gave the audience a dazzling show. For such performers, nothing seemed impossible: it was as if their voices or instruments came alive, and did tricks at their command. The violinist Paganini and the pianist Liszt, for example, played so magnificently that people wondered if they had extra fingers on each hand, or were being helped by unseen assistants, or even by spirits from another world. Showmen-performers like this collected groups of adoring fans, just as pop stars do today.

▼ People enjoyed an evening out at the opera, as well as going to concerts. This painting, by the French artist Degas, shows the opera orchestra (in the pit), and on stage a performance of an opera by the French composer Meyerbeer

▲ While the band plays in the bandstand, some people dance (behind the iron railings) and others eat, drink and watch

19th-century music

Music-making at home was usually a family occasion. Your father or uncle might sing a favourite song; your sister or your aunt might play a piano solo, or join in a duet; the whole family might take part in a sing-song round the piano. People often gave 'musical tea-parties' or 'musical evenings', when family and guests each entertained the others. Sometimes the carpet was rolled back, and everybody danced.

When you went out, the streets were full of buskers and travelling musicians, far more than they are today. You might hear a one-man band, an organ-grinder with his pet monkey, or a band playing on the street-corner.

There was a huge range of musical entertainment: music-hall, dance-hall, pantomime, ballet, opera, and concerts by musicians of every kind, from symphony orchestras to accordion bands.

▼ Barrel-organ and stand

▲ Musical evening: everyone joins in and sings

◀ An organ grinder was a familiar sight on city streets

The 20th century (1900—   )

Music in and out of school

For anyone who likes music, the 20th century is one of the most exciting times there has ever been. Music of all kinds is at your service: turn a knob, press a button, and you can switch from classical to pop, from jazz to ballet, from opera to folk.

But there is more to music than pressing buttons and turning knobs. If you want to make music yourself, there are plenty of opportunities. All through the century, music has been a common subject taught in schools. Most schools have choirs, orchestras, and bands, and there are visiting teachers if you want to learn an instrument.

Outside school, there are private music teachers of instruments and singing, and amateur bands, choirs and orchestras of every kind. You might form a pop group with some friends, join an amateur operatic society, a steel band, or a folk group. Many people find good music-making in their local church.

Most of this music is made as a hobby. If you want to make music your career, there are music colleges, and music courses at most universities, with grants and scholarships to help you pay the fees. Music is a skilled profession, one of the most demanding there is – but it is one of the most satisfying and rewarding, too.

▲ Two 15-year-olds play guitar and saxophone in their spare time

▼ Your great-grandparents might have made music in the drawing room like this group

▲ These students liven up Saturday morning shopping with their saxophones, washboard and concertina

▼ You may have begun learning the recorder at six years old like the children in this photo

▲ A pipe band from a Scottish secondary school

More about
20th-century music B22-9,
    D19-25, E30-2
some 20th-century composers F4,
    F9, F15, F18, F24-5, F30-2

New sounds

The spread of music in the 20th century has meant that all kinds of new sounds can reach our ears. We hear music from all over the world; we have all the fascinating sounds the electronics industry provides. We take for granted instruments our grand-parents never heard of: sitars, guiros, finger-cymbals, claves. We use synthesizers and computers side-by-side with older instruments like guitars and violins. Our ears are stretched: for modern players and composers, no sound seems impossible.

Even so, not all the possible sounds are to everyone's taste, at first. Sometimes, when we hear a new kind of music, we find it disturbing, even ugly. The best answer is to persevere, and see how it sounds when our ears are used to it. Mozart, the piano, waltzing, Frank Sinatra – each of these was regarded as ultra-modern, once. Below, you can read about one new piece that actually caused a riot.

Music is changing and growing all the time. What will the music of the 21st century be like?

◄ The composer Stockhausen setting the controls for a performance of one of his electronic works. You can see an extract from one of his works on page G12 *Writing Music*

More about
Stravinsky F18
The Rite of Spring D27
20th-century music B22-9, D19-25, E28-9, E32
some 20th-century composers F4, F9, F15, F18, F23-4, F26-32

A masterpiece – and a riot

On 15 May 1913, in a theatre in Paris, there was a riot – and it was caused by a piece of music by Stravinsky, a new ballet called *The Rite of Spring*. The story of the ballet tells of some Stone Age tribesmen, who sacrifice a young girl to make sure that winter ends and spring returns. The music suits the story: it is violent, jagged, full of stabbing chords and pulsing drums. Here is part of the last exciting dance:

When the music began, and the curtain went up, the audience at once began to shuffle and whisper. Gradually their noise grew, until they were stamping, shouting, and whistling so loudly that the orchestra was completely drowned. The dancers on stage only kept time because the choreographer stood on a chair at the side of the stage, calling out numbers at the top of his voice, above the roar of the audience.

People began fighting. Those who wanted to enjoy the ballet struggled to silence those who wanted it stopped. The police were called, but not even they could control the audience. The orchestra and dancers struggled on to the end of the ballet; the curtain fell; at that, order was at last restored.

There have often been audience complaints at first performances of new music, both classical and pop. But this riot was one of the largest, and loudest, ever known. Fortunately the ballet company had faith in *The Rite of Spring*. They danced it again, later, and this time scored a big success.

▶ Stravinsky discusses a score with the leader of the orchestra

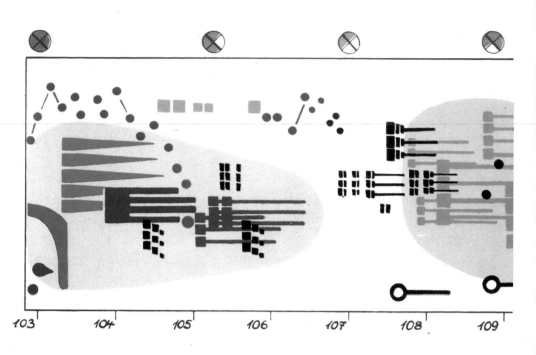

▲ Electronic music. Six seconds from *Artikulation* by the Hungarian composer Ligeti. This piece was made on tape in an electronic studio and the score produced later, the colours representing the sounds

▶ The audience for the last night of the London Promenade Concerts, conducted by Sir Charles Groves, singing 'Rule, Britannia!' (see page E21). The Proms are one of the most important summer musical events in London

▼ Making a record. While the orchestra plays in the studio, an engineer adjusts the balance

Some 20th-century inventions and discoveries

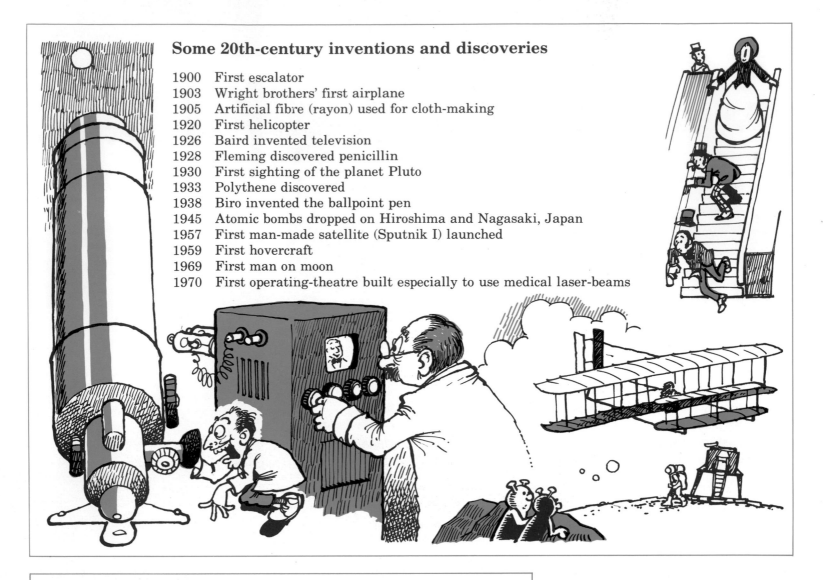

1900	First escalator
1903	Wright brothers' first airplane
1905	Artificial fibre (rayon) used for cloth-making
1920	First helicopter
1926	Baird invented television
1928	Fleming discovered penicillin
1930	First sighting of the planet Pluto
1933	Polythene discovered
1938	Biro invented the ballpoint pen
1945	Atomic bombs dropped on Hiroshima and Nagasaki, Japan
1957	First man-made satellite (Sputnik I) launched
1959	First hovercraft
1969	First man on moon
1970	First operating-theatre built especially to use medical laser-beams

20th-century music

Most of this book talks about the many kinds of music available in the 20th century. Here are a few 20th-century sounds and performers. How many have you heard?

steel band : crooning : ragtime : electronic music : recorder group : jazz band : symphony orchestra : reggae : opera : folk-singing : dance band : rock 'n' roll : brass band : charleston : concert pianist

More about
bands B12-13, B30-2
crooners B21
charleston D19
electronic music C22, G10
folk-singing B2-16
opera D8-17
ragtime B22
reggae B13, B26
recorders E14-15, E29
rock 'n' roll B24
orchestras C24-32
concert pianists C31
jazz B22-23

Composers and their Music

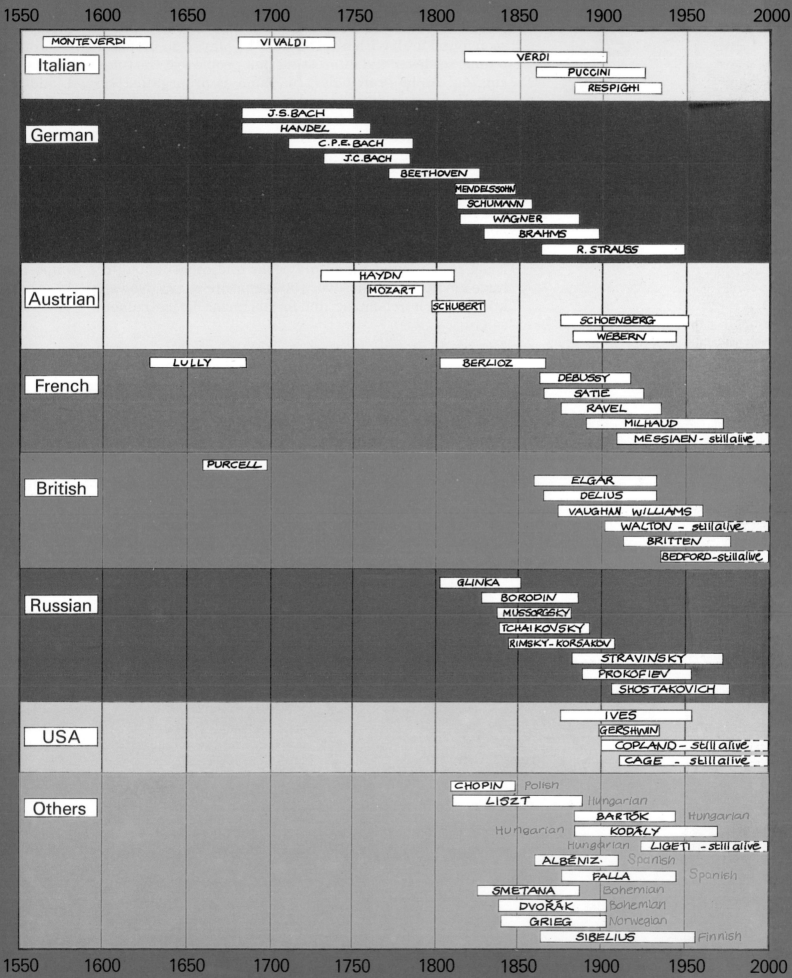

	1550	1600	1650	1700	1750	1800	1850	1900	1950	2000

Italian
- MONTEVERDI
- VIVALDI
- VERDI
- PUCCINI
- RESPIGHI

German
- J.S.BACH
- HANDEL
- C.P.E.BACH
- J.C.BACH
- BEETHOVEN
- MENDELSSOHN
- SCHUMANN
- WAGNER
- BRAHMS
- R. STRAUSS

Austrian
- HAYDN
- MOZART
- SCHUBERT
- SCHOENBERG
- WEBERN

French
- LULLY
- BERLIOZ
- DEBUSSY
- SATIE
- RAVEL
- MILHAUD
- MESSIAEN - still alive

British
- PURCELL
- ELGAR
- DELIUS
- VAUGHAN WILLIAMS
- WALTON - still alive
- BRITTEN
- BEDFORD - still alive

Russian
- GLINKA
- BORODIN
- MUSSORGSKY
- TCHAIKOVSKY
- RIMSKY-KORSAKOV
- STRAVINSKY
- PROKOFIEV
- SHOSTAKOVICH

USA
- IVES
- GERSHWIN
- COPLAND - still alive
- CAGE - still alive

Others
- CHOPIN — Polish
- LISZT — Hungarian
- BARTÓK — Hungarian
- KODÁLY — Hungarian
- LIGETI - still alive — Hungarian
- ALBÉNIZ — Spanish
- FALLA — Spanish
- SMETANA — Bohemian
- DVOŘÁK — Bohemian
- GRIEG — Norwegian
- SIBELIUS — Finnish

1550	1600	1650	1700	1750	1800	1850	1900	1950	2000

Bach

Johann Sebastian Bach (BA-kh). German composer (1685–1750). Bach began his musical life as a choirboy, singing and learning the violin, harpsichord and organ. He also learned to compose. His first job, as a church organist, came when he was 18 – but his employers soon found fault with him, because he played accompaniments for the hymns so clever and interesting that people lost the tune, and stopped singing. As he grew older, his fame as an organist spread, and he travelled widely to play and to teach.

At 38 Bach became director of music at St Thomas's Church, Leipzig, and worked there for the rest of his life (27 years). He was in charge of the music for this cathedral, of music for two parish churches connected with it, and of the music at the University too. He had many pupils (some living with him, boarding in the attics of his house), and his own family was very large: he married twice, and had altogether 20 children.

Bach's house was always full of visitors, full of music and bustle. Even so, he found time (and peace and quiet) enough to compose a huge amount of music: over 1000 separate works. Nowadays he is best known for church music, and for his music for instruments (concertos, sonatas, suites).

▼ Bach at the keyboard, making music with his family

Bach's music

Bach wrote suites and concertos for orchestra (including six *Brandenburg Concertos*), choral music (200 cantatas, two passions, and the *B Minor Mass*), chamber music, and solo music for harpsichord (including the *48 Preludes and Fugues* and *Italian Concerto*), and for organ. Here is the beginning of the Prelude in A flat from Book 2 of the *48 Preludes and Fugues*, as Bach wrote it.

▲ Inside St Thomas's Church, Leipzig

Try the last movement of *Brandenburg Concerto No 2* (a lively piece with a thrilling trumpet part), the peaceful song *Sheep may safely graze*, and the stirring *Toccata and Fugue in D Minor* for organ.

More about
Bach A14, B28, G12, G13
music in Bach's time E18-21

The musical Bach family

Bach was not the only musician in his family. The Bachs had been known as musicians for more than 150 years before he was born. In that time, and for another 100 years, more than 60 Bachs earned their living from music. Some were town musicians, and played trumpets, drums, and violins in processions and for dances. Several, like Bach himself, worked for the church as organists and choirmasters. Bach's father, grandfather, great-grandfather, and several cousins and uncles were all musicians, as well as some of his children.

When Bach's own children grew up, several of them became musicians too. Four of them were composers, and two, **Carl Philipp Emanuel Bach** and **Johann Christian Bach**, were at one time even more well known than their famous father. C.P.E. Bach is remembered today mainly for harpsichord and piano music.

Try the three short, light-hearted movements of C.P.E. Bach's *Symphony Op 3 No 1*, and J.C. Bach's cheerful Rondo in C for piano. (J.C. Bach worked for some time in England, and was nicknamed 'The English Bach'. He was a friend of Mozart's. He wrote symphonies, operas, and piano music.)

▶ Bach's family tree

F3

Bartók

Béla Bartók. Hungarian composer (1881–1945). Bartók's father was the director of an agricultural college. His mother was a school-teacher, and gave him his first piano lessons. There was never any doubt that Bartók would make music his career. At first it seemed that he would be a university professor. He was particularly interested in folk music, and toured the country villages making recordings and noting down the folk music of his native land.

Later, when Bartók became a composer, these studies of folk song affected the whole style and sound of his music. Audiences found it spiky and difficult at first, and he had to earn his living as a piano-teacher and concert pianist as well as a composer. There are many recordings of him playing, both his own music and that of other people.

At the start of the Second World War, Bartók's homeland was over-run by the Nazis, and he decided to leave Europe forever. In 1940 (aged 59) he emigrated to America. He taught at two universities, and composed music for several American orchestras. But he was sad and ill, always homesick for his beloved Hungary. His last compositions are full of the folk tunes and folk music styles he had heard 40 years before, at the start of his career.

▲ A modern group performing the 'Harvest Dance', a Hungarian folk dance. Its tune was probably one which Bartók collected

▼ This cartoon shows how strange people thought Bartók's music sounded

▲ Bartók recording Hungarian peasants and their music

Bartók's music

Bartók's orchestral music includes *Concerto for Orchestra, Music for Strings, Percussion and Celesta,* three piano concertos, and two violin concertos. He also wrote an opera, two ballets, chamber music (including six string quartets), piano music, and songs.

Try the *Rumanian Folk Dances* (either for piano solo, or arranged for orchestra), and the throbbing, clashing first movement of *Concerto for Orchestra.* Here is one of the tunes from it, played on the strings.

More about
music in Bartók's time E28-32
composers and their countries F24

STRINGS

Allegro vivace (Briskly and lively)

Beethoven

Ludwig van Beethoven (BAIT-hoh-ven). German composer (1770–1827). Beethoven's father was a professional musician – and a drunkard. He wanted to turn his son into a child wonder, like Mozart. Every day the boy Beethoven was given many hours of lessons in writing music, and playing the violin, viola, piano and organ. After the age of 11, he learned no other subjects at all. All his life, his maths and handwriting were clumsy and awkward.

He never did become a child prodigy. His fame came later, when he was grown up. In 1792 (aged 22) he settled in Vienna, Austria. Here he made a good living as a concert pianist and composer. He was a favourite in many noblemen's houses, and played concerts, gave lessons, and composed. As a young man he had lessons from Haydn; he also met Mozart, and admired his music.

Beethoven's career as a solo pianist ended in 1802 (when he was 32). His hearing began to trouble him, and by the age of 40 he was almost totally deaf. He could not hear his music played; when people visited him, they had to write their conversation down in notebooks.

The disaster of deafness helped make Beethoven a shy, rather bitter man. He was often sharp and rude, even to his closest friends. He fell into violent rages, for no apparent reason, or stayed silent for days and weeks on end. Even so, he was never short of friends or admirers. For the last 15 years of his life, he was treated as one of the greatest men in Europe. At his funeral, the crowds of mourners were so large that soldiers had to be called out to keep them moving.

Beethoven's music

Beethoven wrote nine symphonies, concertos (including five for piano and one for violin), choral music, an opera (*Fidelio*), and much chamber music (including 16 string quartets and 32 piano sonatas). Here is the tune from the last movement of his Ninth Symphony. It is played first by cellos and basses, then taken up by soloists, choir, and other instruments.

Allegro assai (Quite briskly)

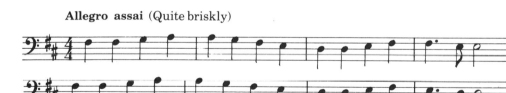

 Try the first movement of *Symphony No 1 in C*, and the rippling *Sonata No 5* ('Spring Sonata') for violin and piano.

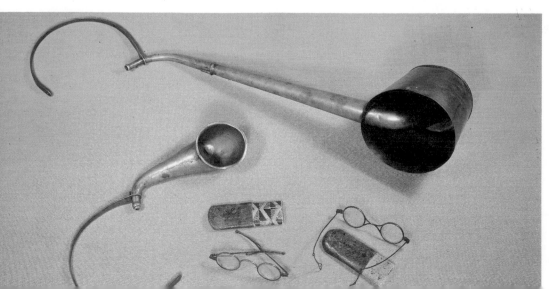

◀ When Beethoven went deaf, he needed ear trumpets to help him hear. You can see these, and his spectacles, at his house in Bonn, now a museum

More about
Beethoven A16, G3, G12-14
music in Beethoven's time
E18-27

Berlioz

Hector Berlioz (BER-lee-oze). French composer (1803–1869). Berlioz's father was a doctor, who wanted his son to learn medicine. But Berlioz ran out in horror from watching his first operation, and gave up medicine forever. All his life he was fascinated by the stage. He married first an actress, then when she died, an opera-singer. He travelled all over Europe conducting his own works, and wrote books and articles on music. He wrote dazzling, colourful music for orchestra, and large-scale operas and masses for voices and orchestra. He believed that music should contain all the feelings and emotions of its composer: for example, his *Fantastic Symphony* tells of the joy and suffering brought by an unhappy love-affair.

Try the overture *Carnaval Romain* ('Roman Carnival'), a bustling, exciting musical picture of people enjoying a public holiday.

▲ This cartoon shows Berlioz conducting in 1846. His tiny wrist movements contrast with the gigantic sounds he is drawing out of his mammoth orchestra. (There is even a cannon with a lighted fuse—pointing in a dangerous direction)

▶ The opening of a section of Berlioz's *Requiem* (Mass for the Dead) as he originally wrote it. Notice how many brass and percussion instruments he uses

More about
music in Berlioz's time E22-7

Brahms

Johannes Brahms. German composer (1833–1897). Brahms's father was a double bass player. He wanted his son to play an orchestral instrument, too. But by the time he was 11, it was clear that Brahms's real gift was for the piano, and so he studied that instead. His family was poor, and as a teenager he had to earn money playing dance music in taverns and dance-halls.

When he was 20, Brahms went on a concert tour of the local towns. He met several important musicians, including the composer Schumann. Schumann wrote an article calling Brahms the finest of all the young musicians, the man the whole world was waiting to hear. This article made Brahms famous, and he and his music were soon in demand everywhere.

In 1863 (aged 30) Brahms settled for good in Vienna, Austria. He lived a quiet life composing, conducting and sometimes playing the piano in public. His hobbies were reading, and collecting old books and model soldiers. He was particularly fond of long country walks, and often used them to work out new pieces of music in his head. He was a shy man, sometimes gruff and rude. But he had many friends and admirers. When he died, the streets of Vienna were crowded for his funeral: the largest such crowds since Beethoven's funeral 70 years before.

All his life, Brahms loved music of the past, particularly the works of Bach, Handel, and Beethoven. His piano practice always included some of the preludes and fugues by Bach, and the suites by Handel; as a young man, he often played sonatas and concertos by Beethoven in his public piano recitals. In his own music, he blended the style of this older music with the newer style of his own time.

Brahms's music

Brahms wrote four symphonies, four concertos, and other orchestral music including *Academic Festival Overture* and *Variations on a Theme of Haydn*. He also wrote vocal music (including *A German Requiem*), much chamber music, and many pieces for solo piano.

Try 'How lovely are thy Dwellings' (from *A German Requiem*), and listen for the tune below, sung by the sopranos of the choir. You might also enjoy the third and fourth movements of *Symphony No 2* (a calm dance followed by an exciting, fast-moving finale).

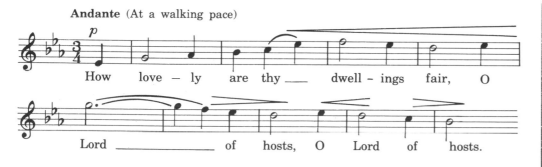

Andante (At a walking pace)

How love — ly are thy ___ dwell – ings fair, O
Lord ___ of hosts, O Lord of hosts.

More about
Brahms A12, A16
music in Brahms's time E22-7

▲ Brahms's favourite restaurant was called 'The Red Hedgehog'. This cartoon shows him (with friend) on his way to dinner

▶ A street scene in Vienna in Brahms's time

Chopin

Frédéric Chopin (SHO-pan). Polish composer (1810–1849). Chopin's father was a professor of French in Warsaw, Poland. Chopin gave his first piano concert at six, and published his first composition at nine. In 1831 (aged 21) he moved to Paris, and made France his main home for the rest of his life.

Chopin was a sensitive, rather shy man, and preferred playing at musical evenings to large-scale, public concerts. Much of his music was written for music-parties like these, or for his piano pupils to play.

Chopin developed the art and style of piano-playing, sometimes fiery, sometimes dreamy and poetic, in a way unknown before. His music is regarded as some of the best ever composed for piano. Many of his pieces are grouped in collections: **mazurkas, waltzes, preludes, nocturnes, scherzos** and **ballades.**

▲ Chopin aged 19 playing for a musical evening at a nobleman's house in Berlin

Chopin's music

Most of Chopin's music is for solo piano (more than 150 works). But he also wrote two piano concertos, chamber music, and a couple of dozen songs. Here is the opening of his *Prelude in B minor* for piano. Notice that the left hand has the tune, while the right hand accompanies.

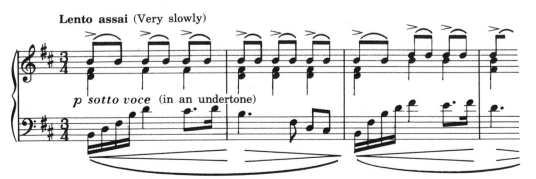

Try *Fantasy-Impromptu Op 66* (a mixture of fast-moving runs and a slow, singing tune), and two pieces nicknamed after their sound, *Raindrop Prelude* (Op 28 No 15) and *Butterfly Study* (Op 25 No 9).

More about
Chopin A12, A14, A16
music in Chopin's time E22-7

Debussy

Claude Debussy (de-bu-SEE). French composer (1862–1918). Debussy's parents owned a china shop. By the time he was eight, it was clear that he had musical talent. He learned the piano, and at 10 began to have lessons at the Paris Conservatoire of Music. While he was there, his interest moved from piano-playing to composing, and he finally won the Conservatoire's main composition prize.

At first, Debussy only just managed to make a living from music. For two years (when he was in his early 20s) he worked for Nadeszhda von Meck, the wealthy lady who also helped Tchaikovsky. He gave piano lessons (he even had to give one on the morning of his wedding, to earn the money to pay for the service).

◀ At the same time as Debussy was composing, a group of painters called *Impressionists* were painting pictures like this one. By using little dots and smudges of colour they tried to give the 'impression' of something; some people thought Debussy was trying for the same effect in his music

Debussy was interested in the music of the Far East, especially the **gamelan** music of Bali. In his own music, he sometimes used sounds and ideas from Eastern music. Many listeners found the new sounds attractive; others thought his music shapeless and strange. He was particularly well known for his piano pieces: many have titles like paintings ('The Isle of Joy'; 'Gardens in the Rain').

Debussy's music

Debussy's orchestral music includes *La Mer* ('The Sea'), *Jeux* ('Games'), *Nocturnes, and Prélude à l' après - midi d'un faune* ('Prelude to a faun's afternoon'). Here are its opening bars, played by solo flute.

▲ Costume designs for Debussy's ballet *Jeux* (Games). The dancers play two kinds of games: tennis, and games of love

FLUTE SOLO

He also wrote an opera, chamber music, songs, and many solo piano works.

🎵 Try his piano pieces *La Cathédrale engloutie* ('The Drowned Cathedral') and *Golliwog's Cakewalk*, and the four short, tuneful movements of *Petite Suite* ('Little Suite') for orchestra.

More about
Debussy A16
gamelan B15
music in Debussy's time E28-32

Handel

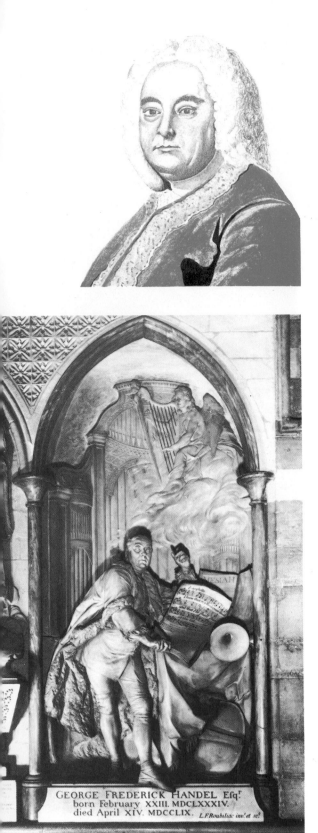

George Frideric Handel. German/English composer (1685–1759). Handel was born in Germany. His father was a barber-surgeon. (In those days, when you did not need advanced medical skills to be a doctor, the same man often did both jobs.) He wanted Handel to be a lawyer, and tried to stop him studying music. Handel only began his full-time musical career after his father's death. He played the violin in an opera-house orchestra, and became quite well known as a solo harpsichord player. Then, aged 20, he wrote his first opera, and began a long and successful career as an opera composer.

Handel moved to London in 1710 (aged 25), and became an English citizen in 1727. His main living was made from operas; but he also wrote choral music and chamber music for rich men. (Good examples are 11 'Chandos' anthems, church music for choir and orchestra, written for his friend the Duke of Chandos.)

When he was 47, Handel began to write an important new kind of work: **oratorios**. These are like religious operas, telling Bible stories in dramatic form. Handel's most famous oratorio is *Messiah* (first sung in Dublin, Ireland, in 1742).

Handel went on playing the harpsichord and organ in public until he was over 60. Then his eyesight began to fail, and for the last few years of his life he was completely blind.

GEORGE FREDERICK HANDEL Esqr
born February XXIII. MDCLXXXIV.
died April XIV. MDCCLIX. *L.F.Roubiliac invt et set*

▲ When Handel died, he was given the honour of being buried in Westminster Abbey. You can still see this monument to him there

◀ The centrepiece for the fireworks display in 1749, for which Handel wrote his *Fireworks Music*.
(This display was exactly copied for the wedding of Prince Charles and Lady Diana Spencer in 1981)

Handel's music

Handel wrote 50 operas, 20 oratorios (including *Messiah*), chamber music, and many concertos and other works for orchestra (including *The Fireworks Music* and *The Water Music*). Here is the well known tune, 'The Harmonious Blacksmith', from one of his Suites for harpsichord.

Andante (At a walking pace)

🎵 Try *The Arrival of the Queen of Sheba* (a bustling piece for strings, with fanfares and chattering trills for two oboes), and the Hallelujah Chorus from *Messiah*.

More about
Handel A11, D6, D10, D14, G13
music in Handel's time E18-21

Haydn

Franz Josef Haydn (HIGH-dn). Austrian composer (1732–1809). Haydn's father was a wheelwright – he made wheels for carts and carriages. Haydn was a choirboy at St Stephen's Cathedral in Vienna, and went to the choir school there. When he was 17, his voice broke, and he had to leave. For the next 12 years he took any job he could find to make a living: teaching, playing the violin and organ, even (for a time) acting as personal servant to another composer (now hardly remembered except as Haydn's employer), Porpora.

In 1761 (aged 29) Haydn became one of the musicians of Prince Esterházy, and five years later he became musician-in-charge. He kept this job for 24 years, until 1790. Haydn was in charge of all the musicians at the Esterháza Palace in Austria (now Hungary). He spent most of his time composing and conducting music for them to play.

After he retired from the service of the Esterházy family, Haydn made his living as a freelance musician, teaching and giving concerts. He made two successful concert tours of England, in 1791 and 1794: the twelve symphonies he wrote for them (six for each) are among his most popular works today. He was respected and loved by musicians everywhere: they gave him the nickname 'Papa Haydn'. One of his friends was Mozart; among his pupils in 1792 was the young Beethoven.

Haydn's music

Haydn wrote music for orchestra (including 104 symphonies), chamber music (including 80 string quartets and 52 piano sonatas), operas, and choral music (including *The Creation* and *The Seasons*). One of his most famous symphonies is 'The Surprise'. At the end of this violin tune in the slow movement, the whole orchestra plays one sudden loud chord, the 'Surprise' that gave the symphony its name.

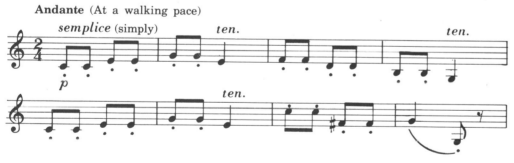

VIOLINS

Try the cheerful last movement of his Trumpet Concerto, the ticking-clock second movement of *Symphony No 101* (nicknamed 'The Clock Symphony').

▲ Haydn playing in a string quartet. He is on the right turning the page

▼ Haydn's visiting-card (which he gave to people when he called on them)

◀ Esterháza Palace, where Haydn spent the greater part of each year. It stands in lonely, marshy countryside, originally part of Austria, now Hungary

More about
Haydn E19, G12, G13
music in Haydn's time E18-21

Liszt

Franz Liszt (LIST). Hungarian composer (1811–1886). Liszt began giving piano recitals at the age of nine. He toured Europe for nearly 40 years, and was one of the most brilliant and successful pianists of his time. He retired as a concert pianist in 1861 (aged 50), and spent the rest of his life composing and conducting instead. He wrote an enormous amount of piano music, most of it in groups of pieces like *Legends*, *Hungarian Rhapsodies*, and *Studies*. As well as piano music, he is well known for several orchestral works, including *The Faust Symphony*, *Les Préludes* ('The Preludes') and two piano concertos.

Try the fiery *Hungarian Rhapsody No 1*, or the calm, rippling *Consolation No 3*.

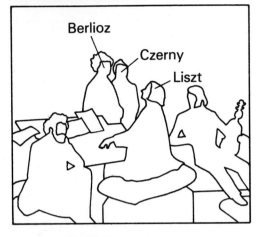

► Liszt playing for some musical friends. You can find out their names from the key above

Lully

Jean-Baptiste Lully. French composer (1632–1687). He worked for King Louis XIV of France. Louis was one of the most dazzling and powerful rulers in Europe. When he was a young man, he appeared in one of Lully's ballets, playing the part of the Sun. Ever afterwards, he was known by the admiring nickname 'The Sun King'. It was Lully's job to provide music for the King's entertainment: ballets, operas and dance-music. He died in 1687, because of a tragic accident. He was conducting a piece of music by banging his stick on the ground (as people did at this time), when he stabbed it into his own foot by mistake. The foot turned septic, and he died of blood poisoning.

Try his dance music for the play *Le Bourgeois Gentilhomme* ('Trying to be a Gentleman').

More about
music in Liszt's time E22-7
music in Lully's time E16-17
Louis XIV D26-27

Mendelssohn

Felix Mendelssohn (MEN-del-soan; his full surname was Mendelssohn-Bartholdy). German composer (1809–1847). Mendelssohn's father was a banker, and a keen music-lover. His house was always full of musicians: there were musical evenings there several times a month. Mendelssohn played the piano at one of them for the first time when he was nine, and began to write music for them soon afterwards. By the time he was 18, he had written symphonies, songs, and piano pieces, several string quartets, and the *Octet* and *Midsummer Night's Dream Overture,* two of his best known and finest works. As well as composing music, he was a good painter. As a grown man, he spent several years in Leipzig, where he was conductor of the famous Gewandhaus Orchestra (still well known today), and director of the Conservatory of Music. He spent time in Britain, where he was a favourite of Queen Victoria. (His *Scotch Symphony* and *Hebrides Overture* are inspired by the scenery he saw in Scotland.)

As well as chamber music and works for orchestra, he wrote a violin concerto, several church works (including the oratorio *Elijah*), songs and piano music (including 48 *Songs without Words).*

🎵 Try the sprightly last movement of his Violin Concerto.

▶ Mendelssohn loved travelling, and sketched in his notebook the places he visited. This is his sketch of Edinburgh Castle, Scotland

Monteverdi

Claudio Monteverdi. Italian composer (1567–1643). He worked for the Duke of Mantua, who loved to listen to singers, and employed many fine soloists and a large choir. Monteverdi wrote church music and madrigals for them to sing. In 1612 he became musician-in-charge at St Mark's, Venice, and spent the rest of his life (31 years) there. He wrote all kinds of church music for St Mark's: masses, motets, psalms. Some of it was in a grand style: there could be three or four choirs and orchestras, performing together from different parts of the church, surrounding the listeners with music. Monteverdi was also one of the first composers of opera, and his operas *Orfeo* (based on the legend of Orpheus), *Ulysses' Return* (based on the Greek legend of Odysseus), and *The Coronation of Poppaea* (based on a story from ancient Rome) are still performed today.

🎵 Try the opening movement of his *Vespers* (1610).

◀ A painting of a religious procession in St Mark's Square, Venice. The magnificent cathedral, where Monteverdi was director of music, is in the background

More about
Monteverdi A16
music in Mendelssohn's time E22-7
music in Monteverdi's time E12-15

Mozart

Wolfgang Amadeus Mozart (MOATS-art). Austrian composer (1756–1791). Mozart's father was a violinist and composer. He worked for a rich nobleman, the Archbishop of Salzburg, in Austria. His job was to provide music for cathedral services, and for the entertainment of the Archbishop and his friends.

Mozart was one of the most musically gifted children we know about. He played the harpsichord at three, began composing at four, and learned the violin when he was six. Because many people of the time were fascinated by 'prodigies' and 'wonder children', his father took him on tours all over Europe to earn money. From the age of six until he was grown up, Mozart spent months of every year travelling, performing for wealthy aristocrats in many countries.

After he grew up, Mozart made his home in Vienna, Austria, and spent part of each year there. But he was often away touring, playing the piano, teaching, and conducting his operas in the musical towns of Europe. This 'freelance' life seems to have suited him better than a fixed, regular job with a single employer – but it also meant that he was always short of money, always working hard to make ends meet. It may also have affected his health – he died when he was only 35.

Apart from money worries, Mozart was a cheerful, happy-go-lucky man. His hobbies included billiards, dancing, skittles, and board games like chess and draughts. He had many friends, and often wrote pieces for their musical evenings, for the particular instruments they played. You can often hear gaiety and happiness in his music, too – sometimes tinged, like his life, with a feeling of sadness.

▲ The six-year-old Mozart playing for the royal family in Vienna

Mozart's music

Mozart wrote 41 symphonies, many concertos (including 27 for piano and four for horn), much chamber music, operas (including *The Marriage of Figaro*, *Don Giovanni* and *The Magic Flute*), and choral music (including the *Requiem*).

🎵 Try the four short movements of *Eine kleine Nachtmusik* ('A little Serenade'). This tune, played by the violins, opens the last movement.

Listen also to the love song '*Là ci darem la mano*' ('Give me your hand') from *Don Giovanni*, and the dancing last movement of *Piano Concerto in A* (K 488).

More about
Mozart A10, A15, A16, D11, G12-14
music in Mozart's time E18-21
Prokofiev A9
Purcell D11, G13
music in Prokofiev's time E28-32
music in Purcell's time E16-17

'K' Numbers

After the name of a Mozart work, you usually see a 'K' number: for example, *Symphony No 40* (K 550). The 'K' number is the number given to the work by Köchel, a 19th-century Austrian writer on music. He made a complete list of all Mozart's works in order of composition. The K stands for Köchel's name, and the number gives the work's place in his list. (Other composers sometimes use 'Opus' numbers. You can read about those on page A14.)

Prokofiev

Sergei Prokofiev (Pro-KO-fee-eff). Russian composer (1891–1953). Prokofiev wrote an opera at the age of nine, and a symphony before he was 12. At 18 he won two prizes with the same piece, his *Piano Concerto No 1*: for composition, and for piano playing (he performed it himself).

Some of Prokofiev's best known music was written for ballets or films: *Romeo and Juliet, Cinderella, Lieutenant Kijé*. He also composed concertos, symphonies (the 'Classical Symphony' is the best known), piano music and songs. *Peter and the Wolf*, a story for speaker with orchestra, is popular all over the world.

 Try *'Troika'* ('Sleighride') from *Lieutenant Kijé*.

Purcell

Henry Purcell. English composer (1659–1695). He worked for King Charles II at the Chapel Royal in London, and was also the organist of Westminster Abbey. Because of his job, he was asked to write music for royal family occasions: weddings, childbirth, funerals, even safe return from journeys. He also wrote music for the stage, church music, and pieces for organ and for harpsichord.

 Try the suite of dances he wrote for a musical entertainment called *The Fairy Queen*.

◄ A scene from Purcell's *The Fairy Queen*, which is based on Shakespeare's play *A Midsummer Night's Dream*

▼ Westminster Abbey, where Purcell was organist

Schubert

Franz Peter Schubert (SHOO-bert). Austrian composer (1797–1828). Schubert's father was a schoolteacher, who was fond of music. As a boy, Schubert learned the violin, viola, piano, and organ. At 11 he won a scholarship to the Imperial choir school in Vienna, and became a choirboy in the Royal Chapel.

When he left school at 16, Schubert became a primary schoolteacher. But he was very bad at it, and gave it up after four years, to concentrate on composing.

For most of his life, Schubert made his living by writing music for the home: songs, piano pieces, music for violin and piano. He also wrote larger works: sonatas, operas, and symphonies. It was harder to make a success with these, and many of them were not performed at all until after his death.

In his own lifetime, Schubert's greatest success was as a composer of **Lieder**, or songs. He composed over 600 of them. He was regarded then (and still is) as one of the greatest song-composers there has ever been.

▼ The beginning of Schubert's song *The Trout*. The right hand of the piano part (the middle line of music) plays swirling, rippling notes to give a musical picture of the 'streamlet' in the song

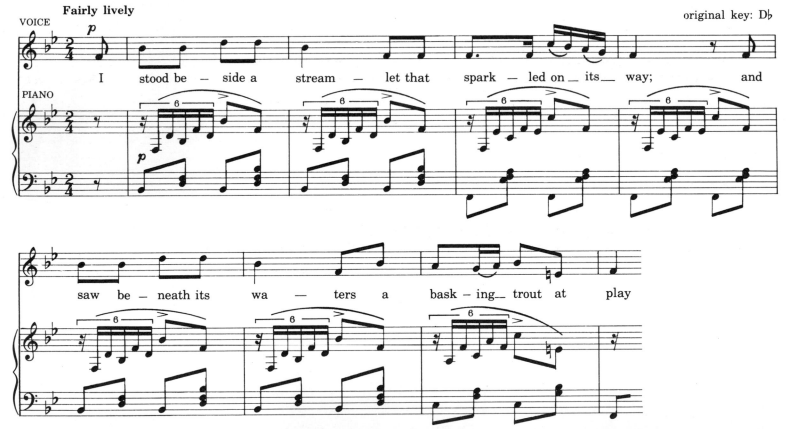

▶ Schubert and his friends setting off for a country drive. He is the man in glasses standing at the back of the carriage

More about
Schubert A10, G12
Schumann A12, A16
music in Schubert's time E22-7
music in Schumann's time E22-7

A 'Schubertiad' at the house of one of Schubert's friends. Schubert is at the piano, ready to play when the party game finishes

Schubert lived all his life in Vienna, Austria. He enjoyed its coffee-houses, its cafés and dance-halls, and the beautiful countryside round about. Most of all, he enjoyed the company of his friends. He had a large group of them, and they spent many evenings together, playing music, singing, dancing, eating and drinking, telling jokes, even juggling and trying out conjuring tricks. Their musical evenings had a special name: **Schubertiads**.

Schubert's music

Schubert wrote music for voices (songs, operas, and choral music), orchestral music (including nine symphonies), chamber music (including the *Octet*), and music for piano solo and piano duet.

Try the song *Die Forelle* ('The Trout'), with its rippling piano part to picture the movement of a fast-flowing stream. You can see some of it printed opposite. Then move on to the cheerful first movement of *Symphony No 5*, and *Marche Militaire* ('Military March') *No 1* for piano duet.

▲ Schubert enjoyed a joke and wrote this piece for violins using cats instead of notes

Schumann

Robert Schumann (SHOO-mahn). German composer (1810–1856). Schumann's father owned a bookshop. Schumann started to learn the piano at eight, and began composing soon afterwards. He went to University to study law, but gave it up for a life of music. He married another pianist, Clara (after his death, one of the most famous piano teachers and performers of the 19th century). He led a busy life, composing, teaching, conducting, playing and writing magazine articles about modern music. He was particularly helpful to young composers: Chopin and Brahms, for example, began successful careers after Schumann described their skill in articles. In 1844 (when he was 34), Schumann's health began to suffer; for the rest of his life he had bouts of nervous illness, and he spent his last few months in an asylum. He wrote symphonies, concertos, chamber music, many songs, and 36 collections of solo music, including *Carnaval* and *Album for the Young*.

Try the short, story-telling pieces of *Scenes of Childhood*, and the slow movement and lively last movement of the Piano Concerto.

Stravinsky

Igor Stravinsky. Russian composer (1882–1971). Stravinsky's father was a famous opera singer. At first he refused to let Stravinsky take up music, and made him study law instead. It was not until he was grown up that Stravinsky could study composing properly. His teacher was the famous Russian composer Rimsky-Korsakov.

In 1910 (aged 28) Stravinsky wrote his ballet *The Firebird*. It was an instant success, and made him famous overnight. In the next 50 years, it became one of his most popular works. He himself worked out that he'd conducted it over 1000 times (that is, an average of once every three weeks for 50 years). He wrote many more ballets. Some (*Petrushka, The Rite of Spring, Apollo, Agon*) are among his best and most exciting works.

As well as being a composer, Stravinsky was well known as a conductor of his own music. He made records of many of his works, and wrote books and articles about music. He was famous for sharp and witty remarks, especially about other musicians. In 1940 (aged 58) he went to live in the U.S.A. His home for many years was Beverly Hills, California, the suburb where many film stars lived.

Stravinsky's music

Stravinsky's most famous ballets include *The Firebird, Petrushka, The Rite of Spring,* and *Pulcinella*. He also wrote orchestral music, operas (including *Oedipus Rex* and *The Rake's Progress*), choral works (including *Symphony of Psalms*) and chamber music. This Russian folk tune was used by Stravinsky in his ballet *The Firebird*. It is played by solo horn in the last scene.

▲ Stravinsky rehearsing the ballet orchestra

The larch tree

Try his tiny joke-piece *Greetings Prelude* for orchestra, the two lively *Suites* for small orchestra, and the mysterious opening of *The Rite of Spring*.

▲ A scene from a modern production of Stravinsky's opera *The Rake's Progress*. The unusual set design is by the modern British painter David Hockney

◄ The moment when the Prince captures the magic Firebird— from an old performance of the ballet

F18

Tchaikovsky

Peter Ilyich Tchaikovsky (chai-KOFF-ski). Russian composer (1840–1893). Tchaikovsky's father was an inspector in the mining industry. At first Tchaikovsky worked as a law clerk for the Russian government, and music was his hobby. Then in 1865 (aged 25), he became a professor at the Moscow Conservatory of Music, and from then on he earned his living as a musician.

At first it was hard to make ends meet. But in 1876 (aged 36) he began an unusual friendship with a rich lady called Nadeszhda von Meck. It was unusual because the two friends never once met face-to-face; instead, they wrote each other letters. Mrs von Meck greatly admired Tchaikovsky's music. For 14 years she paid him a salary to go on composing.

Tchaikovsky's first success, as a composer, was with his operas. Later, his orchestral works became popular, and he toured the world as a conductor. He travelled from Russia as far as Britain and the United States – in those days, long journeys by ship and train.

Three of Tchaikovsky's best works are ballets: *Swan Lake, The Nutcracker* and *Sleeping Beauty*. In his other pieces for orchestra, he wrote the same sort of rich, tuneful music, full of ear-catching instrumental sounds and bright, dancing rhythms.

▲ The house where Tchaikovsky was born. It is now a Tchaikovsky museum

◀ Tchaikovsky is famous for his ballet music. This is a typical scene from *Swan Lake*

Tchaikovsky's music

Tchaikovsky is best known for orchestral music (including six symphonies, the overture *1812*, three piano concertos, and one violin concerto). Here is the tune of the waltz from his *Serenade for Strings*.

Moderato. Tempo di Valse (In waltz time)

dolce e molto grazioso (sweetly and very gracefully)

As well as ballet music, he also wrote 12 operas, chamber music, and songs.

Try his exciting *1812 Overture*, the slow movement and cheerful last movement of his Violin Concerto, and his graceful, swaying *Sleeping Beauty Waltz*.

More about
Tchaikovsky A11, D29, G12
music in Tchaikovsky's time
  E22-7
Stravinsky D27, E30, G2, G11
music in Stravinsky's time
  E28-32

Verdi

Giuseppe Verdi. Italian composer (1813–1901). Verdi's father was the landlord of a small inn. Verdi's first contacts with the theatre were with visiting actors who stayed at the inn. He became a choirboy at the local church when he was seven, and was at first mainly interested in church and cathedral music. But opera soon became his main love, and from the time of his first opera (1839, when he was 26) he spent most of his time writing for the stage. He became one of the finest and most successful opera composers there has ever been.

Some of Verdi's early operas were based on stories from Italian history. At the time, Italy was ruled by Austria, and many people thought that Verdi's operas were really about Italian politics, calling on everyone who loved Italy to help drive out the Austrians and set their country free. In 1860 the Austrians *did* finally leave, and the first free Italian parliament was formed. Verdi was elected an MP, and served for five years. He was honoured as a great Italian patriot for the rest of his life.

In 1870–1871 Verdi wrote his opera *Aida* for the Cairo Opera House in Egypt. Its performance was part of the celebrations for the opening of the Suez Canal. Verdi was nearly 60, and he intended to make *Aida* his last opera. But he loved the works of Shakespeare, and finally agreed to write two more operas based on Shakespeare's plays. *Otello* was first produced in 1887, when he was 74, and *Falstaff* six years later, when he was 80.

▲ Verdi conducting

▶ A scene from Verdi's opera *Falstaff*: Falstaff, who has been writing love letters to Mistress Ford, hides in the laundry basket when her jealous husband appears

Verdi's music

The best known of Verdi's 27 operas are *Rigoletto*, *Il Trovatore* ('The Troubadour'), *La Traviata* ('The Woman who sinned'), *The Force of Destiny*, *Aida*, *Otello* and *Falstaff*. He also wrote a string quartet, and some church music (including the *Requiem*).

🎼 Try the song *'La donna è mobile'* ('Women keep changing their minds') from *Rigoletto*. It is sung by the handsome duke, and begins:

Allegretto (Quite quickly)   original key: B

con brio

Like leaves on   fo-rest trees,   bend-ing to   ev'ry breeze,

legato

Wo-men all   change their minds,   ne-ver   the   same, you'll find

Then try the 'Willow Song' sung by Desdemona in *Otello* just before she dies.

▲ Verdi and his dogs on his country estate

Vivaldi

Antonio Vivaldi. Italian composer (1678–1741). As a young man, Vivaldi trained to be a priest. But he was too devoted to music to make a proper career of the church: sometimes he would even dash out of church in the middle of taking a service, if he had a good idea for his latest piece of music. He travelled all over Europe, playing the violin. (He had fiery red hair, and was nicknamed 'The Red Priest' – very good publicity.) For much of his life he was connected with a girls' orphanage in Venice. Orphans in the 18th century were taught what were called 'useful arts', and these girls had to learn to sing, play instruments, and dance prettily. For all this, Vivaldi provided the music. He wrote operas, chamber music, and hundreds of concertos for solo instruments and orchestra.

🎼 Try the group of story-telling violin concertos called *The Four Seasons*.

◄ Venice in Vivaldi's time. This painting is by the famous Italian painter Canaletto

More about
opera D8
music in Verdi's time E22-7
music in Vivaldi's time E16-17

Wagner

Richard Wagner (VAGH-ner). German composer (1813–1883). As a boy, Wagner went to St Thomas's School, Leipzig, where Bach had once worked. His step-father was an actor, and his sisters opera-singers; he himself spent most of his life working for the theatre, as composer and conductor.

Wagner's first operas were in the usual styles of the time. But soon he began to develop a new kind of his own, called **music-drama**. He wanted to control everything the audience saw – so, as well as composing the music and conducting, he wrote the words, produced, and sometimes designed scenery, costumes and lighting too.

▼ A heroic scene from *The Ring of the Nibelung*, Wagner's most famous music-drama

Wagner's music-dramas were on a huge scale, too big for most ordinary theatres. So, in 1876 (aged 63) he designed a theatre of his own, at Bayreuth (By-ROIT) in Germany. Every year since, at the Bayreuth Festival, Wagner's music-dramas have been performed in the place he intended for them.

▲ Cartoon of Wagner conducting

▶ Wagner conducting Beethoven's Ninth Symphony at a concert in Bayreuth in 1872 to celebrate the laying of the foundation stone of his new theatre

Wagner's music

Wagner's music-dramas are *Tristan and Isolde*, *The Mastersingers*, *Parsifal*, and the four parts of *The Ring of the Nibelung (The Rhine Gold*, *The Valkyries*, *Siegfried*, and *The Twilight of the Gods*). His operas include *The Flying Dutchman* and *Tannhäuser*. He also wrote some chamber music and a few songs.

🎙 Try *Ride of the Valkyries* (a musical picture of warrior-maidens galloping through a storm) and the Overture and Prize Song from *The Mastersingers* (a colourful, pageant-like piece followed by a heroic song). This is the Mastersingers' tune which begins the Overture:

OBOES, CLARINETS, VIOLINS

Molto moderato (Very moderately)

f ben tenuto (sustained)

Walton

William Walton. English composer (born 1902). Walton was a choir-boy, and later a student, at Christ Church, Oxford. His first well known work was written when he was 19: *Façade*. Later, he wrote the music for several films, including *Hamlet* and *Henry V*. His works include concertos for violin, viola and cello, two symphonies, *Belshazzar's Feast*, *Portsmouth Point* and two marches, *Crown Imperial* (for the coronation of King George VI) and *Orb and Sceptre* (for the coronation of Queen Elizabeth II).

🎙 Try the jazzy suite from *Façade No 1*.

▲ Sir William Walton at his home on the island of Ischia, Italy

◀ The coronation procession of Queen Elizabeth II in 1953. Walton wrote the Coronation March *Orb and Sceptre* heard in Westminster Abbey

> **More about**
>
> Wagner D15
> Walton G13
> music in Wagner's time E22-7
> music in Walton's time E28-32

Composers and their countries

When you listen to the music of some composers, it often seems to paint a sound picture of the countries they lived in, as colourful as the souvenirs or photos you bring back from holiday. Many composers used real folk songs and folk dances to give their music a special tang. On these pages is a list of composers' names, and one piece of music each. If you want to hear 'national' sounds, in enjoyable music, these are good pieces to try. Have a good holiday!

Composers

- **Spain**
  Albéniz (1860–1909). *Malagueña*
  Falla (1876–1946). *Ritual Fire Dance*

- **England**
  Delius (1862–1934). *Brigg Fair*
  Vaughan Williams (1872–1958). *English Folk songs Suite*

- **France**
  Satie (1866–1925). *Gymnopédie No 1*
  Milhaud (1892–1974). *Suite Provençale*

- **Scandinavia**
  Grieg – see opposite
  Sibelius (1865–1957). *Finlandia*

- **Czechoslovakia**
  Smetana (1824–1884). Overture, *The Bartered Bride*
  Dvořák – see opposite

- **Hungary**
  Kodály (1882–1967). *Dances from Galanta*
  Bartók (1881–1945). *Rumanian Folk Dances*

- **Russia**
  Glinka (1804–1857). Overture, *Russlan and Ludmila*
  Borodin (1833–1887). *Polovtsian Dances*
  Mussorgsky (1839–1881). *Night on the Bare Mountain*
  Rimsky-Korsakov (1844–1908). *Sheherazade*

More about
Bartók F4
folk music B2-13
Kodály C21
Milhaud A11
music in the 19th century E22-7
music in the 20th century B21-9,
  E28-32

Dvořák

Antonin Dvořák (VOR-shak). Czech (Bohemian) composer (1841–1904).
Dvořák's father was a butcher and innkeeper. As well as composing, Dvořák
studied the organ, violin, and viola. At first he earned his living as a viola-
player in a theatre orchestra. But as his music became known, he was able to
live from composing. He was a friend of Tchaikovsky and of Brahms, whose
music he much admired. In 1892–5 he worked in America, as director of the
National Conservatory of Music in New York. He often visited Britain, and
his music was especially popular with audiences in London, Manchester, and
Birmingham. He wrote a vast amount of music: symphonies, operas, chamber
music, piano music and songs. His best known pieces include the *New World
Symphony, Slavonic Dances*, and the Cello Concerto.

Try the leaping, exciting music of *Slavonic Dance No 1*.

◄ Slavonic dancers today, performing
the high-leaping 'stick dance'

Grieg

Edvard Grieg (GREEG). Norwegian composer (1843–1907).
Grieg's great-grandfather was a Scottish merchant who settled in Norway.
His father ran the family business. Grieg studied music in Denmark and
Germany, and then earned his living as a teacher and conductor in Norway.
One of his main interests was Norwegian folk music: he collected many
tunes, arranged them and used them in his works.

Grieg wrote many songs and pieces for piano. His most famous works
include the Piano Concerto, the *Peer Gynt* suites, *Holberg Suite* for strings,
and *Lyric Pieces* for piano.

Try the short, varied movements of *Peer Gynt Suites Nos 1 and 2*.

▲ Norwegian folk dancers today. Grieg
often used their tunes in his music

◄ Grieg and his wife at the piano

Wizards of the orchestra

One of the most thrilling sounds in all music is made by a symphony orchestra. Some composers use the orchestra like a magician's box of tricks, full of brilliant effects to dazzle and delight the ear.

Many composers deserve the name 'wizard of the orchestra': Handel, Mozart, Berlioz, Wagner, Liszt. But at the end of the 19th century, orchestral playing was finer and more colourful than ever before. The four composers on these pages took advantage of every instrument, every player's skill, in a particularly exciting way.

Mahler

Gustav Mahler (MAH-ler). Austrian composer (1860–1911). Mahler was a famous conductor. He was conductor-in-charge of the Vienna Imperial Opera from 1887–1907 and the New York Philharmonic Society from 1908–1911.

Mahler wrote many songs, often in a folk-song style. Some use piano, others (like *Songs of a Wayfarer*) orchestra. His most famous works are ten symphonies. Several include parts for solo singers and choir, and all need the largest of orchestras. *Symphony No 8* is so vast, and needs so many performers, it was nicknamed 'The Symphony of a Thousand'.

Try the blood-stirring last movement of *Symphony No 1*.

▶ Cartoon of Mahler conducting

Ravel

Maurice Ravel (Ra-VEL). French composer (1875–1937). As well as a composer, Ravel was known as pianist and conductor in his own works. His piano music includes the famous *Pavane pour une Infante Défunte* ('Pavan for a Dead Princess') and three suites, *Gaspard de la Nuit* ('Gaspard of the Night'), *Le Tombeau de Couperin* ('Homage to Couperin') and *Ma Mère l'Oye* ('Mother Goose'). He also wrote chamber music, songs and two short operas.

Ravel's orchestral music includes *Boléro, Piano Concerto in G, La Valse* ('The Waltz') and the ballet *Daphnis and Chloë*. He arranged a good deal of piano music for orchestra, including his own *Mother Goose Suite* and *Homage to Couperin*, and Mussorgsky's *Pictures from an Exhibition*.

Try the majestic *Pavan*, or the jazzy first movement of *Piano Concerto in G*.

Respighi

Ottorino Respighi (Res-PEE-gee). Italian composer (1879–1936). During his lifetime, Respighi's operas were his most successful works. He wrote songs and chamber music, and several popular suites for orchestra. These include *The Birds, The Fountains of Rome, The Pines of Rome,* and a ballet based on music by Rossini, *La Boutique Fantasque* ('The Fantastic Toyshop').

Try the short, bird song-filled movements of *The Birds*.

Strauss

Richard Strauss (Sh-TROWS). German composer (1864–1949). Strauss was the son of an orchestral horn player. He made his fortune as a composer of operas. The most famous are *Rosenkavalier* ('The Rose Cavalier'), *Salome* and *Elektra*. He also wrote chamber music and many songs.

Strauss's most popular music is for the orchestra. He specialized in **symphonic poems** (orchestral pieces that tell a story). Among the most famous are *Don Juan, Till Eulenspiegel, Don Quixote* and *Also Sprach Zarathustra* ('Thus said Zarathustra').

Try the exciting, colourful music of *Don Juan*, or the swaying *Rosenkavalier* waltzes.

◄ This cartoon of Strauss conducting shows him at the top of a huge, sprawling heap of all the sounds and effects people thought they could hear in his music

More about
Ravel A15
music in the 19th century E22-7
music in the 20th century B21-9,
  E28-32
symphony orchestra C24-30

Gallery of 20th-century composers

▲ Britten with his dog by the sea at Aldeburgh, Suffolk, where he lived

Britten

Benjamin Britten. English composer (1913–1976). Britten began composing at the age of 5. By the time he was 12, he had written dozens of works: sonatas, quartets, songs, even an opera. Later, he used some of this music in a grown-up piece, *Simple Symphony*. He is chiefly famous for his operas and songs, and for children's music like *Let's Make an Opera* and *Noye's Fludde*. His best known operas are *Peter Grimes* and *A Midsummer Night's Dream*. His most popular piece of all is perhaps *Variations and Fugue on a Theme of Purcell*.

🎸 Try the first of the Four Sea Interludes from *Peter Grimes*, a musical picture of seagulls hovering over the sea; and the cheerful song 'The Ploughboy'.

Copland

Aaron Copland (COPE-land). American composer (born 1900). Copland decided at the age of 11 that he was going to be a composer. His first success was with a symphony in 1925, and from then on he has been regarded as one of the best of all American composers. His works include the ballets *Rodeo, Billy the Kid* and *Appalachian Spring*, symphonies, songs, and orchestral works like *Quiet City* and *El Salón Mexico*. For someone coming to 'modern music' for the first time, he is an excellent composer to try.

🎸 Try the tuneful 'outdoors' music of the cowboy ballet *Rodeo*.

▶ Characters from one of Copland's cowboy ballets

More about
Britten A9, D12, G13
Elgar G12
music in the 20th century B21-9, E28-32

Elgar

Edward Elgar. English composer (1857–1934). Elgar began his musical career playing the violin in an orchestra, and as an organist and choirmaster in Birmingham. His first great success came with the *Enigma Variations* in 1899 (when he was 42). He wrote two symphonies, concertos for violin and cello, choral works (including *The Dream of Gerontius*), chamber music and songs.

Try the cheerful overture *Cockaigne,* a musical picture of bustling London at the start of the 20th century.

Gershwin

George Gershwin. American composer (1898–1937). Gershwin's main music was written for films, or for the stage. He wrote dozens of hit songs in the 1920s and 1930s (including *I Got Rhythm, S'Wonderful,* and *Summertime,* from his opera *Porgy and Bess*). He also wrote several 'symphonic' pieces: they include *Rhapsody in Blue*, for piano and orchestra, *An American in Paris,* and *Piano Concerto in F*.

Try *Summertime* (sung, if you can get hold of the record, by Ella Fitzgerald); and the jazzy, tuneful *Rhapsody in Blue*.

◀ A violent scene from *Porgy and Bess* — Porgy, the cripple in the centre of the picture, is in love with Bess

Ives

Charles Ives. American composer (1874–1954). Ives always called himself a 'Sunday composer', because for most of his life composing was his hobby. He was interested in unusual sounds (for example, several bands or groups playing different pieces at the same time). He often uses fragments of well known tunes (like *John Brown's Body* or *God Save America*), snipped off and placed in the middle of quite different music. His works include four symphonies, other orchestral music, chamber music, piano music and songs.

Try the loud, cheerful bank-holiday piece *The Fourth of July*.

Messiaen

Oliver Messiaen (MESS-yon). French composer (born 1908). Messiaen is a famous organist as well as a composer. He bases parts of his music on ideas from ancient Greece, the Far East, and the songs of hundreds of birds, which he notes down and rescores for instruments. Much of his music is about the faith and worship of the Roman Catholic Church. He has written orchestral and chamber music, songs, and many pieces for organ and for piano.

Try *Réveil des Oiseaux* ('Dawn Chorus'), a 'birdsong' piece for piano and orchestra.

▲ The piano solo opening, representing a nightingale, of *Réveil des Oiseaux* ('Dawn Chorus')

▶ Messiaen listening to birdsong in the woods and writing it down

Rakhmaninov

Sergei Rakhmaninov (Rak-MAN-in-off). Russian composer (1873–1943). As well as a composer, Rakhmaninov was one of the finest concert pianists of the 20th century. He made many gramophone records, of his own and other people's music. He wrote four piano concertos, three symphonies, operas and chamber music, as well as songs and a large amount of solo piano music.

Try the springy *Prelude in G Minor, Op 23 No 5;* and the colourful *Rhapsody on a Theme of Paganini,* for piano and orchestra.

Schoenberg

Arnold Schoenberg (SHERN-berg). Austrian composer (1874–1951). Schoenberg earned his living as a teacher and professor of music. He wrote music that was so unusual for its time that few audiences understood or welcomed it. Now Schoenberg is regarded as one of the greatest and most important composers of the 20th century. His music has affected the way in which many later composers write. He wrote orchestral music, chamber music, and songs.

 Try the first movement of *String Quartet No 3*.

▶ The composer Schoenberg with some portraits of himself hanging on the wall behind

Shostakovich

Dmitri Shostakovich (shoss-ta-KOH-vich). Russian composer (1906–1975). Shostakovich first studied to be a concert pianist. But when he was 18, his first symphony was a great success, and he decided to concentrate on composing. All through his life, he was regarded as the Soviet Union's leading composer.

◀ Shostakovich and his son Maxim, a conductor and pianist, returning to Moscow from a concert in Leningrad

Shostakovich wrote a vast amount of music: 15 symphonies, 15 string quartets, concertos, sonatas, operas, ballets and songs. His most famous works include *Symphony No 7*, *Symphony No 10* and *Cello Concerto No 1* (written for the famous cellist Rostropovich).

 Try the light-hearted, glittering *Piano Concerto No 2*.

Webern

Anton von Webern (VAY-bern). Austrian composer (1883–1945). Webern was a conductor and a professor of music. His pieces are usually very short, patterns of tiny tunes and single notes like dazzling diamonds (that's how Stravinsky described them). His music was greatly admired by other composers, and his ideas affected the way of writing of almost every important composer since. He wrote orchestral and chamber music, and many songs.

Try the brief, polished *Six Orchestral Pieces*.

More about
Messiaen C21
music in the 20th century B21-9,
E28-32

Three avant-garde composers

Avant-garde means 'ahead of their time'. Composers who are *avant-garde* make sounds that seem strange to many audiences. Sometimes their experiments are soon forgotten; but often they live on, and change the way all later music is written. At one time or another, audiences found Mozart, Beethoven, Tchaikovsky, Stravinsky and Bartók avant-garde.

David Bedford

English composer (born 1937). He has been a schoolteacher, and has written unusual, fascinating music for schools (often mixing ordinary instruments with things like kazoos, rubber bands, combs-and-paper). He often works with pop and rock musicians (especially Mike Oldfield). Like many avant-garde composers, he believes that music can stretch the ears, and still be fun.

Try *Star's End,* for rock instruments and orchestra.

John Cage

American composer (born 1912). He invented the 'prepared piano'– an ordinary piano, with rubbers, pieces of wood, nails and bits of cloth gently pushed against the strings. It makes a distant, unearthly sound, very attractive and very quiet. One of his works, *Radio Music*, is for eight radio sets, tuned to eight different programmes (whatever happens to be broadcast on the day of performance). Another, *Four Minutes Thirty-three Seconds*, consists of total silence – while you listen to it, you can imagine any music you like.

Try the first part of *Concerto for Prepared Piano.*

György Ligeti

Hungarian composer (born 1923). He writes a kind of 'endless belt' music; the sounds go on and on, round and round, with only the tiniest of changes – it's like a river flowing past, with sudden little splashes and whirls in a constantly-moving stream. One of his works is for 100 metronomes (ticking just out of time with one another); another, *Requiem*, uses a chorus who shout, whistle, whisper and hum as well as singing.

Try the cloudy, whispering orchestral piece *Atmospheres.*

▲ Bedford (left); Cage (centre); Ligeti (right). You can see some of Ligeti's music on page E31 of *The Story of Music* and Cage's music on page G10 of *Writing Music*

▼ John Cage's 'prepared piano'. Can you name any of the objects stuck between the strings?

More about
Cage G10
music in the 20th century B21-9, E28-32

Young children in school learning how to read and write music

The composer

▲ Conductor, and composer David Bedford, comparing notes

▼ Stravinsky at his composing-table. (You can see another picture of him at work, on page G11)

Anyone who makes up music is a **composer**. Most people can imagine musical sounds and tunes in their heads; composers are able to pass them on for others to enjoy. Most composers (especially in classical music) write their music down, to show the way they want it performed. Others (especially in pop and jazz) prefer to play it or sing it into a recording machine, and leave it to an **arranger** to write it down and prepare it for the performers to play.

In jazz and pop, what is written down is usually only part of the finished music, the way a skeleton is only part of your body. The performers add the rest, the flesh, when they *improvise*. Most classical music, by contrast, is written out in full, and the performer's job is to play the notes he sees. (Of course, this doesn't mean that he plays like a machine. A good player or conductor tries to match the sounds he creates as closely as possible to the ones he thinks the composer had in mind. That is, he *interprets* the music.) There is a kind of classical music where the players improvise, just as Eastern musicians or jazz performers do. It is called **aleatory music**, or 'music of chance'. In it, the composer provides a skeleton of basic ideas, snatches of notes or chords. But this kind of music is rare: in most classical music, you couldn't improvise without changing what the composer had in mind.

How does the music get on paper?

Most composers begin with rough ideas, the scraps of tune or musical shapes from which a piece will grow. Some composers get ideas by sitting down and thinking; others get flashes of inspiration while doing other things; some work at the piano, guitar or synthesizer, trying over patterns and sound-shapes till the 'right' idea comes.

Once the idea is there, it is often sung into a tape recorder, or jotted down in a rough form called a 'sketch'. Some sketches are short, just a few notes; but there have been composers (Mozart and Schubert, for example) who sketched out whole movements at a time. Beethoven had dozens of notebooks filled with sketches; he used some ideas straight away, but worked on others for months or even years before they became part of finished works.

Once your first ideas are settled, you begin improving and polishing them, and the piece begins to take its final shape. (This is the stage when some composers bring an arranger in.) Every detail is thought about and settled, and a final version is made ready to be performed.

If your music is to be performed soon, you may send it next to the **copyist**. He makes neat copies of each player's part. If it is to be published, the publisher has it printed, and sends you rough copies (called **proofs**) of each printed page. You correct any printing mistakes in the proofs, and send them back. The final copies are then printed, and sent to be sold in music shops.

▲ A page from Beethoven's sketchbook showing his first ideas for the Pastoral Symphony

More about
aleatory music G10
Beethoven F5
interpreting and playing music C29, G7
Stravinsky F18

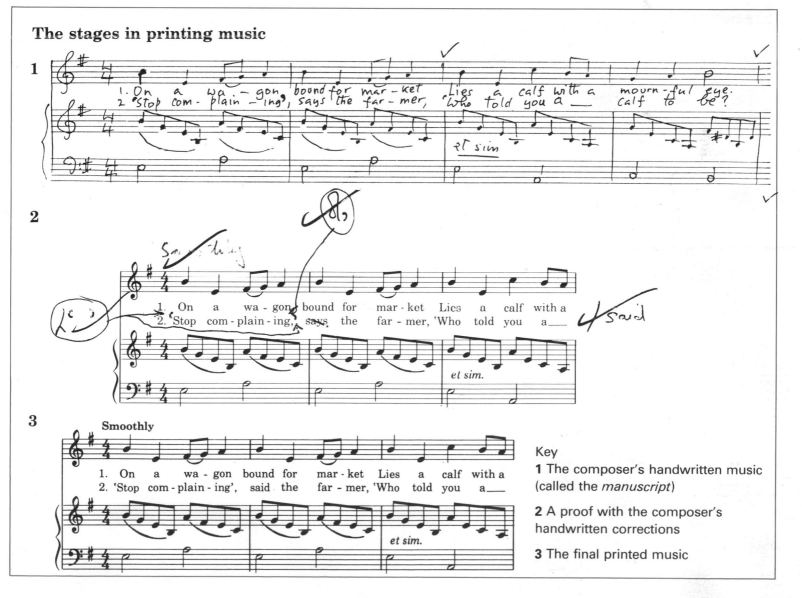

The stages in printing music

Key

1 The composer's handwritten music (called the *manuscript*)

2 A proof with the composer's handwritten corrections

3 The final printed music

Writing music down

When we write words on paper, we are using a kind of code. The letters and sentences tell the reader what thoughts – and sounds – were in the writer's mind. For those who can't read, the signs on paper are a meaningless jumble. But when you have learned the writing code, you can follow its messages, and use it to send messages yourself.

Music writing works in the same way. The signs and marks give a coded message, very easy once you learn to read it. The code tells the performer what sounds were in the composer's mind; the performer interprets the code for the listener, by turning it back into sounds for him to hear.

A composer needs to tell the performer four main things about each sound in his music:

1   How long or short it is
2   How high or low it is
3   What instrument to play it on, or what voice is to sing it
4   How loud or soft it is.

1   How long or short?

Music is made up of single sounds, or notes. When you write music down, you use a different sign for each length of sound. There are whole-note signs, half-note signs, quarter-note signs, and so on. (The length of time a whole note takes is equal to two half-notes or four quarter-notes.)

In America, the different-length notes are given those actual names: whole-notes, half-notes, and so on. In other countries, including Britain, the names are not so obvious; but the table of note-lengths is exactly the same.

American name	Sign	British name
Whole-note	o	Semi-breve
Half-note	♩	Minim
Quarter-note	♩	Crotchet
Eighth-note	♪	Quaver
Sixteenth-note	♪	Semiquaver

sixteenth-notes (semiquavers)

eighth-notes (quavers)

quarter-notes (crotchets)

half-notes (minims)

whole-note (semibreve)

Speed

As well as sorting out the length of each note, most composers also say how fast or slow they want the whole piece to go. Usually they do this by putting an Italian word at the beginning of the music – a word meaning 'fast', 'slow', or 'moderate'. (Italian is used because the idea of describing speed in words began in Italy, and once the words were used, they stuck.) Musicians all over the world, even if they don't speak Italian, use the same words for musical speeds. On page G7 you can see a box of the words most often used.

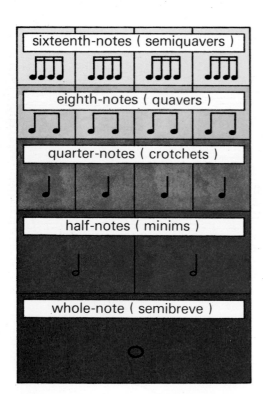

Metronomes

The trouble with using *words* for speed is that they are not exact. How fast is 'fast'? If you walk 'fast', is it the same speed as when your friend walks 'fast'? If a piece of music is to be played 'fast', how can the composer make sure that people will always play it at his chosen speed?

One answer is a **metronome**. This is a kind of clock which can be made to tick a measured number of times every minute. You fix it to tick at the speed the composer asks, get the speed in your head, turn the metronome off and start to play. Metronomes are never used in concerts – their ticking would disturb the music. But musicians often use them at home, when they begin to learn a piece.

At the start of a piece of music, you may find an instruction like this: ♩ = 120. It means that the composer wants a speed where 120 crotchets (or quarter-notes) are played every minute. You fix the metronome at 120 ticks a minute, and so find out the exact speed to play each crotchet.

Metronomes were invented at the beginning of the 19th century. The early ones were clockwork. Nowadays there are electronic metronomes as well: instead of a tick, they sometimes give a buzz.

▲ Clockwork metronome

▼ Electronic metronome

2 How high or low?

Music is written on groups of five lines. (There used to be more, but five is as many as the eye can easily read at once.)

$$\left. \begin{array}{c} \text{——} \\ \text{——} \\ \text{——} \\ \text{——} \\ \text{——} \end{array} \right\} \text{stave}$$

Each group of five lines is called a **stave**. Each line or space on the stave means one particular note. The space at the bottom is the lowest note, and the spaces and lines move up one note at a time.

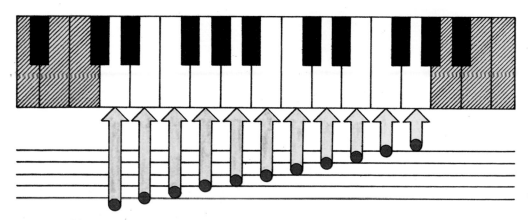

To tell you which line means which note, a sign called a **clef** is used. This fixes the note for a particular line. Once that line is fixed, all the others are fixed as well. Each stave has only one clef on it at a time.

The treble clef is used for high voices and instruments. It normally curls around the next-to-bottom line of the stave. That line is then fixed as G, and the other lines and spaces follow up or down from there.

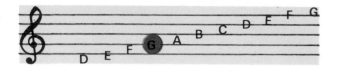

Treble or 'G' clef

The bass clef is used for low voices and instruments. It normally goes on the fourth line up. That line is then fixed as F, and all the other lines and spaces follow on.

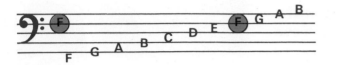

The C clef is rarer than the others. It is usual in viola music, and is sometimes used for cello, bassoon, and trombone music too. The line it goes on is fixed as C. The C clef is called the **alto clef** if it goes on the middle line, and the **tenor clef** if it goes on the fourth line up.

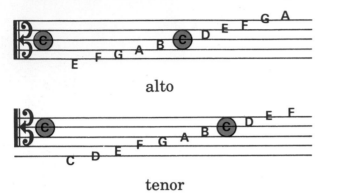

alto

tenor

Bass or 'F' clef

'C' clef (alto or tenor clef)

3   What instrument?

The composer writes the name of each instrument at the beginning of its line of music. If only a few instruments are used, the names are left out after the first line. In more complicated music (like the piece by Beethoven on pages G8-G9) there may be names at the start of each new page. This saves the conductor getting confused.

◀ The opening of the slow movement of Haydn's Trumpet Concerto. As you can see, the instruments playing here are flute and strings

4   How loud or soft?

Italian words are used to show how loud or soft the music should be played. Sometimes you use the whole word; sometimes just the first letter is enough. One page G7 you can find a box of common words, with their meanings.

Signs can be used as well. The commonest are

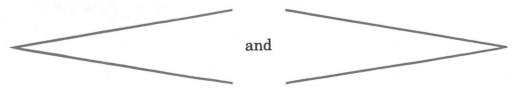

and

(meaning *crescendo*,
kre-SHEN-doh, 'get louder'),

(meaning *diminuendo*,
dim-in-you-EN-doh, 'get softer').

The performer

Speed, loudness and softness, the *way* you play each note – for each of these things, the written music gives a clear guide. If you are a performer, a main part of your skill is making decisions about all these matters, presenting the music in the way you think it will sound its best. No two performers make exactly the same decisions, perform the same piece in exactly the same way. Even if we know a piece well, a new performer can make us hear things in it we've never heard before.

Some words for loud and soft

Letter	Italian word	Pronounced	Meaning
pp	pianissimo	pyan-IS-si-moh	very soft
p	piano	PYAN-oh	soft
mp	mezzo piano	MET-zoh pyan-oh	fairly soft
mf	mezzo forte	MET-zoh for-tay	fairly loud
f	forte	FOR-tay	loud
ff	fortissimo	for-TIS-si-moh	very loud

Some words for fast and slow

Italian word	Pronounced	Meaning
adagio	ad-AH-gee-oh	very slow
lento	LEN-toh	slow
andante	an-DAN-tay	slow walking pace
allegretto	al-lay-GRET-toh	brisk walking pace
allegro	al-LAY-groh	fairly fast
vivace	viv-AH-chay	fast
presto	PRES-toh	very fast
accelerando (accel.)	a-chel-er-AN-doh	getting faster
ritardando (rit.)	rit-ar-DAN-doh	getting slower

Mood words

These suggest to the performer the kind of feeling the composer wants in the music.

Italian words	Pronounced	Meaning
con brio	kon BREE-oh	with spirit
espressivo	es-press-EE-voh	expressively
furioso	foor-ri-OH-soh	rushing
giocoso	jo-KOH-soh	playfully
grazioso	grats-i-OH-soh	gracefully
marcato	mar-KAH-toh	with emphasis
pesante	pe-SAN-tay	heavily marked
semplice	SEM-plee-chay	simply
tranquillo	tran-QUEE-loh	peacefully
vivace	viv-AH-chay	lively

More about
interpreting and playing music C29, G2
writing music down G4-6, G8-10

An orchestral score

The pages of music that contain a whole piece, when they are grouped together, are called a **score**. The score contains everything necessary to tell the performers how to play the music. When musicians talk of 'scoring' a piece of music, they mean writing it down complete in every detail.

Opposite is a page of score from Beethoven's *Symphony No 5*. It shows the beginning of the fourth movement. This is an **orchestral score**: it shows the parts for all the instruments, and contains every detail.

The following instruments play the *tune*: piccolo, 1st flute, 1st oboe, 1st clarinet, 1st bassoon, 1st horn, 1st trumpet, 1st trombone, and violins. (The violins play other backing notes as well.) So many instruments play the tune that it sounds loud and triumphant, the main thing you hear. The instruments playing *harmony* (the 'backing' that supports the tune) are: 2nd flute, 2nd oboe, 2nd clarinet, 2nd bassoon, 2nd horn, 2nd trumpet, 2nd trombone, and violas. The *bass* line is played by these instruments: double bassoon, bass trombone, timpani, cellos, and double basses.

Key

1 The instruments are always grouped this way in an orchestral score: woodwind at the top, then brass, percussion, and strings. As you can see, some lines of music are for two or more instruments: in the flute part, for instance, the first flute player plays the top notes of each pair, and the second flute player the bottom notes. 'Zu 2' (bassoon part, bar 4) means that both players play the same notes.

2 Allegro (♩ = 84). This tells the conductor that the movement should be played fairly fast. If he checks his speed with a metronome, it should tick 84 minim beats every minute.

3 ff. At the start of the movement, all the instruments are playing very loud.

4 Most of the instruments use the **treble clef**. The lowest-sounding instruments use the **bass clef**. Two kinds of instruments use the **C clef**: high trombones and violas.

5 These little dots show that these notes are to be played *staccato*, that is, cut off short almost as soon as they are sounded. How short is 'short'? That's one of the things the conductor must decide.

6 These lines are a **repeat sign**. Later in the movement, there will be another one. When it comes, the musicians go back to this one, and play all the music in between again.

7 This letter C is a **time-signature**. It tells the conductor how many beats in each bar. Some time-signatures are figures (for example, $\frac{3}{4}$ means three crotchet beats per bar). The letter C stands for **common time**, that is, four crotchets to each bar.

8 Rests. These tell the players not to play. Each rest, like each note, has a definite length.

More about
instruments of the orchestra C2-23
the symphony orchestra C24-30
writing music down G4-7, G10

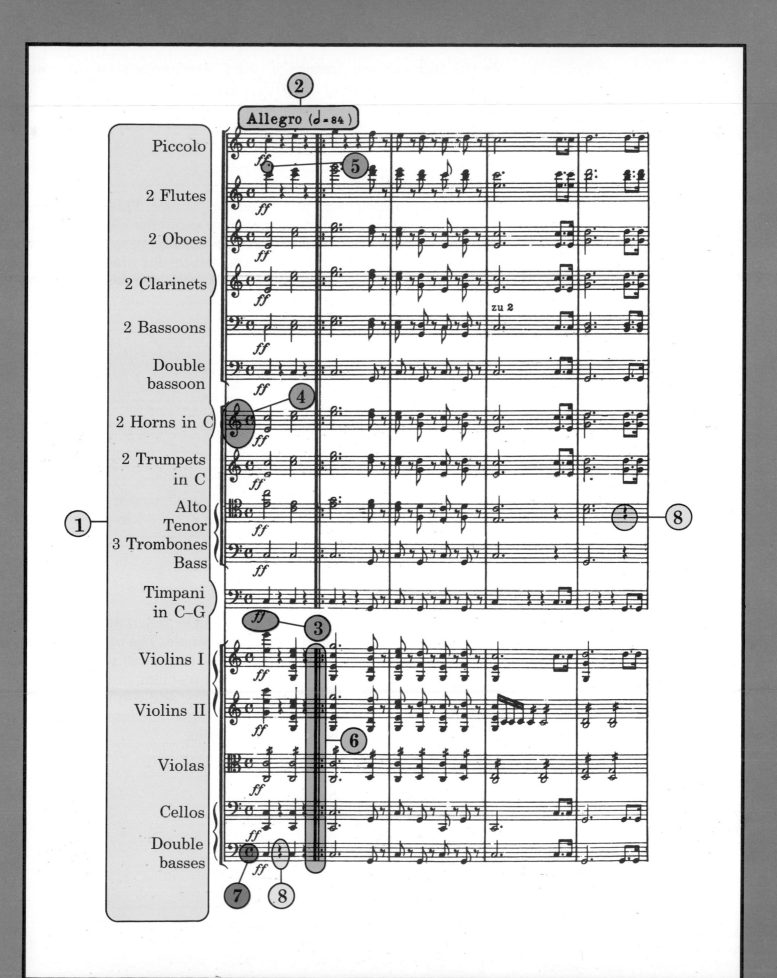

▲ 16th-century tablature for the lute, and (below) modern tablature for the guitar

▶ Aleatory music: part of *Concert for Piano and Orchestra* by the American composer John Cage. Each shape suggests an 'island' of notes round the main note printed

Unusual kinds of score

Tablature

In the 16th century, instead of using lines and spaces, composers of lute music used a method called **tablature**. They wrote the music down in the form of numbers: diagrams showing where the player's fingers should go on the strings. This method is still used for guitar-chords in many song-books today.

Aleatory music

Many modern composers write **aleatory** music. This leaves the performer free to make up parts of the music as he goes along. He can vary the sounds as he chooses, and the composer's score is meant only as a guide to the sounds he should make. Scores for aleatory music are rather like pictures of sounds, meant to excite the performer's imagination as he begins to play.

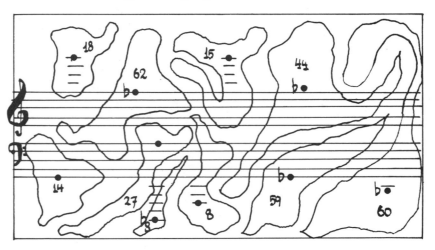

Electronic music

In electronic music, the sounds are made by machines (synthesizers, modulators, tape-recorders) instead of people. The operator who controls the machines needs to know how long each sound lasts, and which switches or knobs to use at each moment in the piece. Many composers work the machines themselves, and use no scores. When scores *are* made, they often look like graphs or computer print-outs, with shapes and symbols instead of notes.

▶ Electronic music: The opening page of the score of *Studie II* by the German composer Karlheinz Stockhausen. This was the first electronic work to appear in print. You can see a picture of Stockhausen on page E30, *The Story of Music*

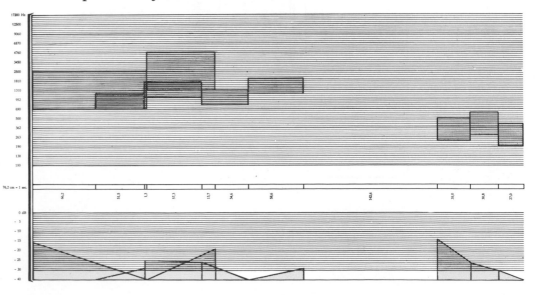

What kind of piece?

When a composer sets to work, he usually has some idea of the kind of piece he means to write. His music may be on a large scale – an opera, or a musical, say, with several hours of music written for dozens of singers and an orchestra. Or it may be simpler – a song, say, or a solo for just one instrument. He needs to know what singers or players will be available, the sort of music they want (simple? tuneful? sad? with words? with a lively beat?), and sometimes even the places where it will be performed (no one writes orchestral music for a living room, or a high-kicking dance for church).

Pop song-writing is different. The words may be written first, or they may come later, once the tune is there. The composer makes up a tune, and writes it down or sings it into a tape recorder. When the basic tune is ready, other parts are added (by an arranger, or by other members of the pop group), until the music is complete. Most songs are short; long works (like rock operas) are made up of many separate songs.

A classical composer's music may be for church, stage, orchestra or soloist. Each branch of classical music is different, and has different musical needs. When you write a classical piece (say a symphony or an opera), you can invent a completely new way of doing it – or you can follow ways other composers have used before. On pages G12-14 are some favourite ways, with listening suggestions if you want to explore them for yourself.

◀ Stravinsky composing, in his sunny California garden. (You can see him indoors on page G2)

> **More about**
> lute music E14-15
> electronic instruments C22
> writing music down G4-9

Music for orchestra

Overture (OH-ver-ture)

A short piece (usually about 5–15 minutes long) for orchestra alone. Some overtures are taken from operas or plays. The word 'overture' really means 'opening piece', and the overture was the first music you heard as the show began.) Others (called 'concert overtures') are not connected with the stage, and were written especially to be used in the concert-hall. Usually the music of an overture tells a story (like Tchaikovsky's *1812 Overture*, which includes a battle), or gives a musical impression of a painting, a poem, or a scene from nature (like Mendelssohn's overture *Fingal's Cave*).

Try the two overtures mentioned, and Malcolm Arnold's overture *Tam O'Shanter*. For each of them, try to find out the story first (perhaps from the record sleeve). Tam O'Shanter, for example, is an exciting tale of a man who raced a pack of witches, who were trying to snatch his soul away.

Suite (SWEET)

Several short pieces or movements grouped together. Many suites are taken from ballet music or the music for plays (for example Delibes's *Coppélia* suite or Elgar's two *Wand of Youth* suites). Others were written for concerts, and have no other connections.

Try the Air from Bach's *Suite No 3* (sometimes called *Air on the G String*), the overture from Fauré's suite *Masques et Bergamasques*, and the *Coppélia* suite and *Wand of Youth* suites mentioned above. Holst's suite *The Planets* makes exciting listening, especially the movements called 'Mars, Bringer of War', and 'Jupiter, Bringer of Jollity'.

Symphony (SIM-fo-ni).

This is one of the largest, most important kinds of classical music. Like a suite, a symphony has several movements. But the music is usually much more closely connected, more serious. Many symphonies have four movements: a large opening movement, often in quick time; a slow, song-like movement; a dance-like movement, often a minuet (min-you-ET) or a faster scherzo (SKERT-so); and a last movement or finale (fin-AH-leh), usually on a large scale to balance the first movement. For many composers, writing symphonies was one of the most challenging jobs there was; the symphonies of Haydn, Mozart, Beethoven, and Tchaikovsky are among the finest orchestral works of all.

To begin with, it's a good idea to take symphonies one movement at a time. The first movement of Mozart's *Symphony No 40,* and the last movement of Haydn's *Symphony No 101* are good ones to hear first. Then try the 'Waltz' from Tchaikovsky's *Symphony No 6* – a good waltz to listen to, but impossible for dancing, as it has groups of 5 beats instead of the usual 3. If you want to move on to a complete symphony, try Schubert's *Symphony No 5*.

You can read more about how symphonies began on page E20.

More about
Bach F2
Beethoven F5
Elgar F26
Haydn F11
Mendelssohn F13
Mozart F14
orchestras C24-7
Schubert F16
Tchaikovsky F19

Music for voices

Cantata (can-TAH-ta)

The word cantata was once part of the Italian phrase *musica cantata* ('sung music'). It means a piece for solo voice or voices, sometimes with choir. The accompaniment can be for a few instruments, or an orchestra. Handel wrote many solo cantatas: they are to dramatic words, and are like tiny operas for a single voice. Bach wrote cantatas for church use: their words are religious, and the music often includes the tunes of well known chorales.

Try Mozart's cantata *Exsultate, Jubilate* (K 165), a joyful, triumphant piece for solo voice and orchestra. Listen to *Jesu, Joy of Man's Desiring*, from Bach's Cantata No 147. If you enjoy it, move on to Cantata No 140.

Mass

The Mass is the main service in the Roman Catholic Church, and many composers have written masses for church use, and also for performance in the concert-hall. In a musical mass, there are five sections, each using part of the service words. The sections are known by Greek or Latin names: *Kyrie* ('Lord have mercy on us'), *Gloria* ('Glory be to God'), *Credo* ('I believe in God'), *Sanctus* ('Holy, Holy, Holy'), and *Agnus Dei* ('Lamb of God, have mercy on us'). As well as ordinary masses, many composers have written Requiem Masses, that is, masses in memory of the dead.

Begin with Britten's bouncy, rhythmic *Missa Brevis* ('Short Mass') for boys' choir and organ, and the movement *Dies Irae* from Mozart's *Requiem*.

Oratorio (OR-a-TOH-ri-oh)

Rather like a religious opera, with soloists, choir and orchestra telling a story from the Bible. (The main difference is that oratorios are not acted on a stage like operas: they are performed at concerts, in churches or concert-halls.) Like oratorios are **Passions**, usually performed in church at Easter. These tell the story of Christ's death and resurrection, using the words of the Bible. Like cantatas, they often use well known chorale tunes.

Try the Christmas section from Handel's *Messiah*. If you enjoy that, listen to the rest of the work. For a colourful, exciting modern oratorio, try Walton's *Belshazzar's Feast*.

Other kinds of choral music

As well as the music mentioned above, which uses mainly religious words, there are plenty of choral works using ordinary words. Often they were written for special occasions, like Purcell's *Ode on St Cecilia's Day* (to celebrate November 22, the day of the patron saint of music). Some composers wrote **choral symphonies**, adding soloists and a choir to the usual orchestra. Beethoven's *Symphony No 9*, and Vaughan Williams's *Sea Symphony* are two of the best known. (The main tune from the last movement of Beethoven's symphony is used as the European National Anthem.) As well as these kinds of music, choirs often sing shorter works like folk song arrangements and **madrigals**.

Begin with short pieces: Vaughan Williams's *Just as the Tide was flowing*, and Britten's *A Ceremony of Carols*. For longer works, try a short sample first, and move on to a complete performance. Britten's *Noye's Fludde* and *St Nicolas* are fun, and Orff's *Carmina Burana* (begin with the section called *Spring*) is full of tuneful, rhythmic music – you might like to contrast it with the quieter, more thoughtful style of Haydn's *The Creation*.

Music for soloists

Concerto (con-CHER-toh)

A piece of music for soloist and orchestra. Concertos normally last for 20–40 minutes, and many have three movements: fast, slow, fast. In most concertos, the music is written to show off the beauty and skill of the soloist's playing. As well as concertos for one solo instrument, there are a few **double concertos** (for two) and **triple concertos** (for three).

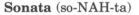 Try single movements first. Good to begin with are Litolff's *Scherzo for piano and orchestra,* and Saint-Saëns's *Introduction and Rondo capriccioso for violin and orchestra:* the names are long, but the pieces are light and full of bubbling tunes. For complete concertos, try Mozart's *Horn Concerto No 4,* and Rodrigo's *Guitar Concerto* (sometimes called by its Spanish name, *Concierto de Aranjuez).* Movements from each of them are well known on their own; but they sound even better when you hear the works complete.

Sonata (so-NAH-ta)

A sonata is a piece of music for soloist alone, or for solo instrument and accompaniment (usually piano). The word sonata comes from the Italian phrase *musica sonata* ('music to play'). Since Mozart's time (the end of the 18th century), most sonatas have had four movements, sometimes three. Some are short, lighthearted pieces; but many are longer, more serious works, almost like symphonies for solo instrument. Many composers have also written **sonatinas** (son-a-TEEN-as, 'little sonatas'). These are usually shorter and easier to play than full scale sonatas, and you often use them when you learn an instrument.

Try first Mozart's *Piano Sonata in A minor* (K 331). It begins with variations on a nursery-rhyme-like tune, goes on to a beautiful slow minuet, and ends with a march, in which Mozart gives a piano impression of drumbeats, clashing cymbals, and piccolos playing running decorations high above the tune. After that, try Beethoven's *Spring Sonata* for violin and piano, and his *Sonata Pathétique* ('Sonata full of feeling') for piano alone. Poulenc's *Sonata for flute and piano* is graceful and lighthearted, well worth tracking down.

More about
Bach F2
Beethoven F5
Britten F28
church music D5-7
Handel F10
Haydn F11
madrigals E15
Mozart F14
Rodrigo C13
Vaughan Williams F24
Walton F23

Index

a

accompaniment A12, D4, see backing
acoustics A12
Africa B10-12
air A12
Albéniz F24
aleatory music G2, G10
alto clef G6, G8
alto voice D4, D7
anthem D7
aria A12
Arnold A10, G12,
arranging music G2-3

b

Bach, C.P.E. F3
Bach, J.C. F3
Bach, J.S. A14, B28, D6, E19, F2-3, F7, G12, G13
backing A12, C27
background music B5, see incidental music
bagpipes B30-1
ballad E21
ballade A12, F8
ballet D26-32, E30
bands B13, B22-3, B30-2
baritone (brass instrument) C10
baritone voice D7
baroque music D10, D18, D20, E16-17
Bartók F4, F24
bass clef G6, G8
bass voice D4, D7
bassoon B31, C4, C6, C24
beating time C29
Beatles A15, A25, B28, C27
Bedford F32
Beethoven A16, B6, B14, E20, E24, F5, F7, F11, G3, G8-9, G13-14
Berlioz E24, F6
Bizet D12
Borodin F24
Brahms A12, A16, E26, F17, F25, G13
brass bands B32
brass instruments B23, C7-10, C24
Britten A9, D12, F28, G13
Bronze Age E5
bugle C10
buskers B17
Byrd E12

c

Cage F32
calypso B12
canon A12
cantata G13
celesta C21
cello C12, C24
chamber music C32
Chant D6
Charleston D19
China B15-16, E4
choirs C26, D5-7, G13
Chopin A12, A14, A16, F8, F17

chorale E17
chord A13
choreographer D30
chorus D8
church music A16, D5-7, E8-9, E12, E17, see religious music
cimbalom C13, C21
clarinet B22-3, B31, C4, C6, C24
clavichord C19
concert master C28
concerto A14, C31
concerts C26, C28, E20, E26-7
conductor C28-9, D13
contralto D7
Copland F28
cornet B31-2, C10
Couperin E16
crooning B21
cymbals B31, C16

d

dance notation D32
dancing B2-4, B7, B10, B16, D18-32
Debussy A16, F9
Delibes D28, G12
Delius F24
divertimento A13, A15, E21
divertissement D27
double bass B22-3, C12, C24
double bassoon C6, C24
drums B10-11, B13, B16, B22-3, B30-2, C15-16
duet C32
Dukas A10
dulcimer C13
Dvořák F24-5

e

Egypt, Ancient D5, D4-7
eighteenth-century music D10, D18-20, E16-21
electronic instruments C22
electronic music E31, G10
Elgar F29, G12
euphonium B31-2, C10

f

Falla F24
falsetto D4
fantasia A13
Fauré G12
fiddle A13
films B21, B27, D23-5
finale A13
flute B16, B22, C4-5, C24
flute, walking stick C23
folk music B2-13, D18
folk rock B26
foxtrot D19, D20
fugue A9, A14

g

Gabrieli E12
galliard D20, E14
gamelan orchestra B15, F9
Gershwin F29

Gilbert and Sullivan D16-17
glasses, musical C23
Glinka F24
gong B16, C16
Gounod E25
Greece, Ancient D5, E4-6
Grieg F24-5
guitar B22-3, C13, G10

h

Handel A11, D6, D10, D18, E20, F7, F10, G13
harp C17, C24
harp, Aeolian C23
harpsichord C18, E16
Haydn D6, E19, E21, F5, F11, G12, G13
hit B20-1
Holst G12
horn B10, B31, C7-8, C24
hymn D6-7, E17

i

improvising B14, B22, G2
incidental music C27, see stage and theatre
India B14-15, E4
instruments G6
Ives F29

j

Japan B15
jazz B22-3, G2
jive D21
jive, hand B24

k

'K' number F14
kettledrum (timpani) C15-16, C24
keyboard instruments A14, C19-23
Kodály C21, F24

l

Lassus E15
leader C28
Lehár D16
libretto D13
Lieder F16
Ligeti F32
listening to music A9-10, D15, G7, G12-14
Liszt E25, E26, F12
Litolff G14
Lully E17, F12
lute E14, G10
lyric A14

m

madrigal E14-15
Mahler F26
manual A14, C20
maracas C16
march A9
masque E17
mass G13
medley A13
melody A14
Messiaen C21, F30
metronome G7, G8